What Others Say about UPI

When I was in the Atlanta Braves farm system I was fortunate enough to meet Tim Cash with UPI. Tim invited me to do a clinic with some of the Braves players and other former players who love the Lord. At that time I was a young Christian who had never shared the gospel through a baseball clinic. I saw firsthand the difference UPI can make for Christ. Tim Cash challenged me to grow. His zeal for Christ was second to none. I admired his boldness and every time I have a chance to be around a person who is on fire for the Lord, I get excited. Over the years I've had the privilege of meeting Mickey Weston and Tom Roy, and God has used them to influence so many by their willingness to share the gospel with others. God has used UPI to make a difference in the lives of so many. I'm glad God put UPI into my life.

Rich Maloney, *Head Coach, University of Michigan Baseball*

When everybody seems to be catering to baseball players, UPI goes after the heart and gives an eternal perspective on *what really is important*. Without UPI, I would not be the person I am today.

John Smoltz, *All-Star pitcher*

When you talk about the great teams in sports, you have to include the group at UPI. C̶ d Brian Hommell have been nothi̶ exactly coaches…more like sheph ̶ize and embrace God's plan for m̶

Ernie Johnson, *studio*

I have seen firsthand the impact that God is having through Tom Roy and the ministry of UPI and it is special. Whether it is the personal encouragement and friendship of Tom or being able to minister together to our armed service men and women in places around the world, lives are being changed and the kingdom is advancing.

Aaron Kampman, *All Pro defensive end, Green Bay Packers*

Now that I have reached the magic 70 milestone, I am even more appreciative of having met Tom some 28 years ago in Oliver, British Columbia. Game Changer! I would never want to forget the six memorable years of baseball camps in Tsawwassen, British Columbia, where the UPI Team changed so many lives. Unforgettable time only because of the talents and efforts of Tom Roy. Tom could join our Bible study tomorrow and be greeted as a member. Hardly a week goes by that I don't bring up something Tom said or did that is such an important part of my life. He is a true brother in Christ!

Don Dell, *UPI camp host; father of a pro ballplayer*

UPI serves two vital roles in relationship to baseball; first, it provides wise and godly input in the lives of active professional players and uses those contacts to, second, minister the gospel to those around the world through baseball clinics and training camps. UPI also provides me personally with friends who are interested and hungry to keep abreast with new developments in theology. This kind of hunger and interest is rare in the church and yet it is throughout the staff at UPI. May God continue to bless and prosper this vital outreach ministry.

Mark H. Soto, *D. Min., Professor of Biblical Studies and Director of Online Education, Grace Theological Seminary, Winona Lake, Indiana*

There are two words that have described UPI for me...Tom Roy. He has personified being trustworthy, loving, honest and compassionate. Ministry without the personality of Jesus would be religion. UPI without the character issues I laid out would be just another nonprofit enterprise.

Joe Urcavich, *Chaplain, Green Bay Packers, Senior Pastor, Green Bay Community Church*

Tom Roy and UPI started out ministering to a small segment of society—professional baseball players and their families. This ministry has grown over the years to include youth, members of the armed forces, and others. He and they remain singularly effective at communicating the Good News across this wide spectrum with selfless conviction and humor.

Col. John Sullivan, *Director, ServantLeader Ministries, author of* Servant First! Leadership for the New Millennium

How do I summarize all that UPI has meant to me? These men have tremendously impacted my life and taught me what it "looks" like to be a true Man of God. Tom Roy is the man that I spent the most time with, learned the most from, and to whom I owe most of my growth as a Christian man. These men invest time, energy, prayer, and love into all they do, and we are all greatly blessed because of them. I truly love these men and am eternally grateful.

Tony Graffanino, *MLB player*

UPI has been a spiritual resource and spiritual guidance in a very worldly profession. The friendships and community provided by UPI are most needed in the game of life.

Sal Bando, *MLB player and general manager*

UPI has served in Europe as an icebreaker between Christians and the sports world. Their passion and expertise for the game are evident. With seriousness and humour, with courage and creativity they add some special flavour to the rich baseball culture. Tom Roy personifies what seems to be the success formula of UPI: to be real, to be close enough, and to have clear communication. Wherever I met Tom somewhere in the world, I found him full of passion and love—a real friend and a man of integrity.

Hermann Guehring, *President, International Sports Coalition*

It's been my privilege to watch Tom Roy and UPI for over twenty-five years. In this time, God has blessed UPI's mission because they are solidly committed to exalting Christ and His Word. I know firsthand that they take these commitments seriously and the effects of what God has done through UPI are evident worldwide. I am one of countless numbers through the years who have been touched by UPI's love for God, for His truth, and for people. And I am grateful.

Dr. Les Lofquist, *IFCA International Executive Director*

As a female athlete, it is refreshing and encouraging to see a ministry like UPI helping men discover that their identity is not in their sport or awards on the diamond, how high they were drafted, whom they date/marry, how much money they make, what car they drive, or in any other thing of this world, but in Jesus Christ. UPI truly desires to walk alongside and disciple men in what it means to be a man after God's heart, whose identities are wrapped up in Him. The UPI staff and volunteers are genuine in their desire to see lives transformed as they meet these players where they are, and I am blessed to have them as brothers in Christ and partners in ministry. Thank you, UPI for the ministry you do day to day.

Nicole Rapagnani, *Fellowship of Christian Athletes, and former women's rower at the University of Notre Dame*

It's been incredible to see how God has used UPI in kingdom-building, not only here in this country, but all over the world. The result: Hearts have been touched, lives changed, and souls saved!

Scott Sanderson, *sports agent and former MLB All-Star pitcher*

I can't express how much UPI means to me. Umpiring is a profession of isolation, and the men of UPI are my lifelines. Tom is a man I rely on for solid biblical guidance and a whole lot of laughs.

Tom Barrett, *MLB umpire*

Released

BMH Books
www.bmhbooks.com
Winona Lake, IN 46590

Released
A Story of God's Power Released in Pro Baseball

ISBN: 978-0-88469-269-0
RELIGION / Christian Ministry / Discipleship

Published by BMH books, Winona Lake, IN 46590
www.bmhbooks.com

UPI offers a special note of appreciation to The Arington Foundation for their support in this publishing venture.

Dedication

To my wife Carin and our daughters, Amy and Lindsay,
who have experienced with me the joy and pain of ministry.
Without their understanding of the mission
God has given our family,
this work would have been short-lived.

I love each of you very much!

Table of Contents

Foreword

We are so used to open doors that we often take the power of God for granted. In the fourteenth chapter of Acts, Paul and Barnabas returned to Antioch and reported to the church all that God had done through them and how he had "opened the door of faith to the Gentiles."

New Testament figures such as Paul are larger than life to many of us. Tom Roy reminds me of a modern day Paul in many ways—a bold leader who is faithful to his calling and, most importantly, has a strong and consistent walk with Jesus.

Acting on the vision God laid out for him, Tom and the men who have joined him over the years have impacted countless lives around the world for eternity. Serving Christ through baseball sounds simple enough, but Tom and the Unlimited Potential staff have trusted God to open doors around the world.

I witnessed this ministry firsthand on a trip with UPI to Hong Kong and China, and it has impacted my life. How blessed we are to have freedom to follow Christ, which we tend to take for granted. In China we didn't pray publicly; instead we sat around a table with our eyes open and had "conversation." I came home from that trip with an appreciation for the sacrifices made by those who leave the comforts of our Western culture to serve on the foreign mission field.

Tom Roy has been a very close friend since the early 80s and a ministry partner nearly as long. His desire in writing this book is to show the power of God at work in and through those who serve our Master Jesus in this unique ministry. He not only shares the highlights, but opens up about some of the disappointments and what God has taught him over the years. Whether or not you are passionate about baseball or missions, this book will be entertaining, informative, and encouraging.

Vince Nauss, *President, Baseball Chapel*

Preface

In 1980 God put it on my heart to share the gospel of Christ through the vehicle of professional baseball. My vision was to reach the world through the platform of the player, because the entire world needs to hear the life-changing message of salvation by faith in Jesus Christ. Players have bought into this passion—players who knew what they believed and were not afraid to speak about it.

Most people are enamored with the players and their larger-than-life careers. Many ballplayers are looking for something bigger than their own careers. Unlimited Potential Incorporated (UPI) became a ministry specifically to and through baseball personnel. UPI cooperates with Baseball Chapel and Pro Athletes Outreach (PAO) to minister to pro baseball players and to provide platforms for Christian players to reach out around the world to speak about their faith.

These are real life stories, demonstrating that even when we fail, God is at work. Even when our faith is feeble, He shows up. This is the account of how God has reached into the lives of world-class ballplayers and used them to impact the world.

Tom Roy, *Founder/President, UPI*
Philippians 3:10
December 2009

We will not conceal them from their children,
But tell to the generation to come the praises of the LORD,
And His strength and His wondrous works that He has done.

(Psalm 78:4 NASB)

A Strange Call

"Hon, the phone's for you."

"Who is it?" I asked, absorbed in my TV program.

"Hank Aaron," Carin responded.

"Yeah, right!" I said, under my breath.

It was January 1978, during one of the worst blizzards in Indiana history. The snow had blown a large drift against our front door, roads were closed, and most businesses were shut down. I wasn't going anywhere.

At that time I worked for Huntington College (now Huntington University) in the admissions office. I was also the pitching coach for the baseball team. Days were long and my travel schedule was packed. It was nice to have an unscheduled day off!

As an assistant coach, I had suggested a kick off event for our upcoming baseball season. We needed to do something to show people that basketball was not the only sport in Indiana. Huntington's baseball team was a powerhouse in the state at the NAIA level and Head Coach Jim Wilson and I wanted to raise interest in the community. We decided a named celebrity would draw a crowd. My responsibility was to come up with the celebrity.

I had no real contacts inside major league baseball—just a keen interest in the game. How would I find a baseball celebrity that would come to Huntington, Indiana? I began making a list of celebrities, including Ernie Banks of the Chicago Cubs, Stan Musial of the St. Louis Cardinals, and Hank Aaron, the home run king of the Atlanta Braves. I sent out letters to the teams of these "stars of the past."

"Hon, Hank Aaron is on the phone for you," my wife repeated after I had not responded to her the first time. Carin was not one for practical jokes, so I thought maybe she heard the name wrong. I got up from my comfortable chair and took my time getting to the phone.

"Hello, this is Tom Roy," I said.

"Yes, Tom. This is Hank Aaron. I received your letter and was calling about the speaking possibility at Huntington College." It really was Hank Aaron, my childhood hero!

Growing up in the small town of Grafton, Wisconsin, just outside of Milwaukee, I knew who Hank Aaron was. I remembered many evenings with my ear to the transistor radio, listening to the Milwaukee Braves. The Braves were Milwaukee's team and Hank Aaron was the star.

In 1978, Aaron had retired from baseball as an active player and had signed a contract as a spokesman for the Magnavox Corporation, headquartered in Fort Wayne, Indiana, about 25 miles from Huntington.

Aaron mentioned that he traveled to Fort Wayne often, and I gathered my thoughts enough to discuss details like the date, location, and honorarium. Hank Aaron agreed to be our speaker. Needless to say, I was pumped. I called Coach Wilson to tell him the news and we both knew that something special had just happened.

A month later I was standing in the Fort Wayne airport, waiting for the arrival of my hero. When he walked off the plane I was stunned…he showed up. I tried to act natural as we waited for his bag and loaded the car for the short drive to his hotel. On the outside I hope I appeared calm. But on the inside I was going 100 mph.

During the drive to his hotel, Aaron patiently answered my questions about his flight and his life after baseball. The Ft. Wayne airport is located in a rural area outside of Ft. Wayne, and it was not easy to get to the hotel on the other side of the city—at least for me. Carin will tell you I am not blessed with a great sense of direction–no internal GPS. After about 40 minutes of driving, Hank politely asked me if I had any idea where I was going. The truth was I was lost and had no clue how to get to the Hilton. Humiliated, I stopped at a gas station to ask for directions—a true sign of weakness in a man.

I knew Aaron just wanted to get to his hotel and relax after the flight, and we were still 30 minutes away. Figuring I had already lost all credibility with him I decided to ask one more question. "Do you have any spiritual roots?" I asked.

Without hesitation he began to tell of his childhood years and his first trip to pro ball on a train. With only a pair of baseball spikes in his bag, he left his hometown to start his career in pro baseball. He talked of his family's spiritual roots and how God was important to him. He then directed the same question back at me. I wasn't prepared for that, but I gulped and began to tell him my story.

I had been released by the San Francisco Giants organization after a very short time in pro ball. My dream of being a major league baseball player was shattered. I left depressed and searching.

I told him how a girl I dated had talked to me about a personal relationship with Jesus. I was raised in church and knew that Jesus loved me, that I was a sinner, and that His death on the cross paid for my sin. But she said eternal life was a gift of God received by faith, not by earning it with good works (Eph. 2: 8-9). I told Aaron that I had asked Jesus Christ to take over my life.

Wow, I had just been given the opportunity to express my faith to my hero, and he had listened. In fact, he more than listened, he connected. It no longer mattered that we were lost and miles from his hotel. We were deep into a conversation about life and faith.

When we finally arrived at the Hilton, we stayed in the car another 10 minutes, finishing our conversation. He asked if I would join him for dinner later that evening to continue our talk.

That night during dinner I acted as his bodyguard. People recognized Hank and wanted autographs. I asked them to please allow Aaron to eat a meal in private. (I kind of felt like a big shot.) We had a great conversation between the constant interruptions.

Later that evening we drove to the Huntington College gymnasium for the event. As an introduction, we showed a short film of Aaron appearing in an All-Star game. He and I were sitting in the athletic director's office on the second level of the gym. The office had a window overlooking the gym and we turned out the lights to prevent reflection.

As we watched the film together in the darkened room we were joking and punching each other as we anticipated the next hitter. We watched as Hank hit a home run and we cheered. For a brief moment we were kids again, just loving the game.

When the film was over, we turned the lights on and straightened our ties. It was show time. We walked to the platform together.

In our phone conversation, Hank had told me he would speak for only 30 minutes—no question and answer session. I agreed. Who was I to tell Hank Aaron what he could do?

As I remember that evening, he did a wonderful job of speaking, describing what it was like to chase Babe Ruth's record. He talked of the media hype, the interviews, lost sleep, racial slurs, even death threats, as well as moments of great joy. It was a special evening and I think even Hank knew that he had hit another long one with this audience.

Then he surprised me. He turned to me and said, "I'll take about fifteen minutes of questions." Yes, he had connected with the audience and felt free to be even more open. None of us was prepared for the first question.

A college girl raised her hand with a question: "Mr. Aaron, what did Jesus Christ mean to you during your quest for the home run record?" I was stunned. Hank turned around and gave me a look that said, "Did you plant this girl in the audience?" Then I saw a gleam in his eye, as he turned and answered the question. He mentioned that he and I had just had a good discussion about religion. He continued to talk about how God was important in his life.

That encounter with Hank Aaron has had a huge impact on my life. Getting lost while driving to his hotel had humbled me. But because of that I had been able to talk about what meant most to me with a man who was my childhood hero, and it touched him at a deep level.

If a man like Hank Aaron was willing to listen, why not share Jesus Christ with other players? It wasn't about me; it was about *the message*. My spiritual wheels were put into motion. What was God showing me?

As a baseball coach, my theme was "Great to be alive!" It became the team motto and motivator.

It's Great to be alive because God is in control!

Action Points

- Have you ever plotted out your life timeline—the highs and lows of your life?

- Has God intersected your life at any time? What did that look like?

- Have you ever considered sharing your lifeline with someone you love or trust (a good friend or family member, for example)? It just might do you and them good!

Tom Roy with Hank Aaron

Baseball Culture

In 2007 more than 79 million fans attended Major League baseball games. Again, in 2008, despite a sagging economy, the number was over 78 million.[1] Add to that the many who listened on radio or watched games on TV, and you have an idea why baseball is called America's game. The game can captivate you. Young and old alike talk about their heroes and highlights of the game. Perhaps it's the personalities in the game; the skinny pitcher who talks to the ball, the base-stealing champion who frames and hangs his bonus check on the wall without cashing it or the basket catches of the "Say Hey" kid. Others rehash bad plays and talk about how the game was played the right way when they were young. There were those summer days spent sitting in lawn chairs grilling burgers and listening to the favorite team on the radio. With today's technology, fans can follow their favorite teams anywhere in the world. Either way, there is a love of the game.

Why is there this fascination with a game? Could it be the history? Or could it be the fact that many have played the game at some level, from Little League to city league to church softball? Maybe

---

[1] bizofbaseball.com. The 2008 Major League Baseball regular season was the second highest attendance mark in history, drawing 78,624,324, falling just 1.14 percent below the previous year's record of 79,502,524 in paid attendance, a sign that baseball's popularity remains exceptionally strong. While the figure is the second best ever, forecasts at the beginning of the season were for a total attendance in excess of 80 million. Still, the strong attendance figure comes at a time when the economy has been hit exceptionally hard, gas prices impacted travel, and the weather wreaked havoc at open-air stadiums, lowering walk-up ticket purchases.

it is because of the unique features of the game. For example, did you know that baseball is one of the only games in the world where the defense gets the ball? That makes it a totally different experience from soccer, basketball, or football.

I was one who followed the game. The Milwaukee Braves were my team. Growing up in the 50s and 60s, I had memorized each player's position and stats, as well as most of the other National League players. I would spend hours standing in our gravel driveway and do "play by play" in my head as I tossed up a stone and hit it into the field behind our house. Over the years, I wore down the surface of the driveway as I dreamed of becoming a big league player. I would also spend hours playing wiffle ball with my brothers and the neighbors.

Signing with the Giants in 1967 was a dream come true for me. But hitting stones in the driveway or playing church softball is a long way from pro baseball. Pro baseball is not just about the big contract or the baseball cards or even the fame. It is a business. It is about production. If you don't produce, you go home. It is also extremely tough on families. Let me give you a glimpse from the inside.

Imagine you are 18 years old, and you receive a phone call in June from a major league team. The voice represents a team that has just drafted you, and within a few days a scout will arrive at your home to have you sign your first professional contract. Pretty exciting! When the scout arrives, he is courteous and seems happy for you. He tells you what an honor it is to play professional baseball and that many kids around the world would love to be in your position. After a few minutes of small talk and pleasantries with you and your family, he pulls out the contract.

If you were drafted in the first round, you are an instant millionaire. Each first-round player is given a signing bonus. It is money up front that says the team has the rights to you. They have drafted you high because they expect you to make it to the big leagues. The first pick in the draft can sign for a multi-million dollar bonus. Others signed in the first round will likely get a million dollar-plus signing bonus, but the numbers are negotiable. Most high draft picks hire an agent to negotiate the money. Sometimes the amount is determined before the draft, but usually the negotiation process begins after the player is drafted.

If you are drafted in the first 10 rounds, you probably receive $10,000 or more in signing bonuses. In recent years the signing bonuses have increased since young players need that money to live on for the years they spend in the minor leagues. If you sign lower than the tenth round, you will most likely get a small signing bonus. Below the twentieth round, well, you get a handshake and a "good luck."

Now you are a professional baseball player. Starting pay for any player in his first year is $1,100 per month before taxes.[2] This salary is paid for only five months, and no pay is given during spring training. In addition, each player pays monthly clubhouse dues. Players have to share apartments with inflated seasonal rates or find housing with a family in town. I have seen minor league players sharing a fourth floor apartment with no elevator, no furniture, and no air conditioning. You sign as a hero and live like a pauper.

Professional baseball has levels you must move through before getting to the major leagues. You begin in Rookie ball and move to Low A, Middle A, High A, Double A and Triple A before finally making it to the major leagues. That is much different from football or basketball where a drafted player goes immediately to the top level. There is a reason for the long journey to the big leagues. There is a lot to learn and a lot of experience to gain as you climb the ladder.

Pay increases a little each year but not by much. By the time a player reaches AAA the first time, he is guaranteed to make $2,150 per month. The numbers change if he has had time in the big leagues and is sent down, but for the first-year player in the minors, the pay is predetermined. Needless to say, minor league players eat at the kind of restaurants where one does not have to tip. If he should make it to a major league team, the first year pay is $390,000. If he is only there for a portion of the season, the pay is prorated.

Another factor to consider is that a minor league player has few rights. He is the property of the team until he has played six years for an organization. The team can trade him, move him, call him

---

[2] Source for salary information from minorleaguebaseball.com.

up, send him down, or cut him during those first six years. After six years, he becomes a free agent and can negotiate with other teams.

Although you play for a team, you are not really a team. There is a saying in baseball: "You are a corporation of one." Organizations move players up to the next level one by one, not by teams. It is no longer high school or college ball; you are on your own. If your team wins a championship in the minors, you may get a ring and a few good memories, but only the best players will move to the next level. You are evaluated on what you have done as an individual.

If you finally make it to the "show," the fun really begins. Suddenly the size of the crowds increases greatly, along with the expectations. There is the pressure of the ever-intrusive media. There is the daily battle to hold onto your position. If you don't perform, there is someone waiting to take your place. You are trying to beat the player ahead of you as you watch out for the younger players coming up below you. The money is good, but when your salary is public knowledge it adds to the pressure to produce. There is also the constant possibility of a trade or an injury. There are few professions with more uncertainty.

Baseball, for the most part, is a second-shift job. You typically play night games, arriving at the park between 1 p.m. and 3 p.m. every day and leaving after midnight. You play 162 games during the regular season, plus 25-30 games in spring training. If your team makes it to the playoffs, the number of games increases. It is very physical work—a blue-collar job with white-collar pay.

Minor league teams often travel by bus and stay in mediocre hotels. One day a minor league coach told me about a hotel he was in at the minor league level. He had his son along, and the first night in the hotel he found bug bites all over his son's body. You never know what the hotels will be like. The minor league stadiums have really improved over the years, but they are not the same as the big league parks. The playing surfaces can be vastly different.

There is also a huge difference in the way the players are treated. The higher up the chain you go, the more perks you receive. Big league players are given free meals, cars, clothes, and more. Minor league players get very little. It is the love of the game and the dream of making it to the big leagues that make players willing to live with the inconveniences of minor league ball. Statistics show that for every hundred athletes who sign a contract to play professional baseball, only three make it to the major leagues.

Next, imagine being married while playing in the minor leagues. First, your wedding needs to be planned for the off-season. There are few days off in baseball. Once you are married, your wife will probably have to work since the two of you can't live on your income. That means you will be separated from February until the playoffs end in the fall. If you can afford to be together during the season, she will be alone during the frequent road trips. It is not an easy life for couples, but your dream becomes her dream.

Let's say your dream of making it to the big leagues has come true. You are making a nice salary and life is good. You are one of the few. But the average big league player does not last three years. You are able to use the first few years, if you make it that long, to pay off some of the debt that has multiplied during your time in the minors. But there are expectations of what life will be like in the big leagues. You have finally made it. You may feel you deserve to spend your money on the vehicle, vacation, or vice you have imagined. How quickly that salary can disappear.

For those who are gifted and remain healthy, there is a big paycheck waiting. But remember, the better your career goes, the less personal life you have. Who can you trust? Why do people want to get close to you? You question their motives for friendship. Do they want something from you or do they just want to use you to their own advantage? People you haven't heard from in years suddenly become your new best friends. Relatives need a loan, friends need a favor, and others approach you with "great investment opportunities."

Life in the big leagues can also have its challenges for the player's wife. She is the one who usually handles all the details of life so he can play the game. She shares her husband with the public, but she does not share in his fame. She sits in the stands with the other wives and knows her husband is competing for the same job as the husband of the wife next to her. She tries to lift her husband's spirits if he is struggling in the game. She feels pressure to be thin, fit, and well dressed. She knows there are always women waiting outside hotel rooms and locker rooms, willing and available to ballplayers.

Imagine yourself as a player's wife. You wake up one morning to read in the newspaper that your husband's job has been eliminated. He's been traded to a team on the opposite coast. He has to leave immediately and be ready to play the next day. He boards a plane and looks for a hotel to stay in until he can get settled. For the next few days he will try to navigate his way around the city and develop some relationships with new management and teammates. But what about you? You are left to pack all your belongings, close all your accounts, shut off the utilities, sub-lease your apartment, and move across the country. Then you have to find housing and begin again in a new city. If you have children, you have to arrange for schooling.

That is the life of a professional baseball player. Most players make a minimum of three moves a year. They usually have a location they call home, a second location for spring training, and a third place to live during the regular season. Once a player is established in the big leagues with a good salary, it makes the process a little easier. But most do not ever make it to the big leagues. There are many who are called up or sent down, traded, sent to play winter ball, or asked to play in extended spring training, requiring multiple moves each year.

It is a privilege to be able to play pro baseball. Few men have the opportunity to do what they truly love. A big league contract comes with many perks, such as a new vehicle to drive, a contract with a sports apparel company, endorsement contracts, travel opportunities, and the chance to meet many celebrities. But with privilege comes pressure. There are few professions where your job performance is broadcast on national news every day, where your neighbor can read your salary in the paper, or where your kids are ridiculed at school if you had a bad game. There are few careers that are as short-lived as professional baseball.

Baseball is not all glory. The pressure can be great, and the life-style can be tough on marriages. This is just a glimpse into the life of a pro baseball player, and it is into this culture that UPI is bringing the message of Jesus Christ, a message of meaning and hope. It is a message that gives a new perspective on life, a message that God is in control, even in the uncertainty of the baseball lifestyle. He loves pro athletes for who they are, not for their performance or position. But why would God call me to a ministry within the baseball culture?

It's Great to be alive because God is in control!

Action Points

- Take some time today to think about the unique challenges that are part of your life and profession.

- List the pressures you feel to perform well.

- How do you react to and handle praise or criticism?

- Who do you turn to when the pressures seem to mount, and no one seems to understand?

Called Up

Throughout history God has called people from all over the world, with various backgrounds and skills, to be on His team. Carin and I were just a young couple from Grafton, Wisconsin, a small town near Milwaukee. Later God would draft others to the ministry of UPI from towns like Newnan, Georgia; Flint, Michigan; Bemidji, Minnesota; Kokomo, Indiana; and Hutchinson, Kansas. This book is about God's birthing and shaping Unlimited Potential, Inc. (UPI), a unique baseball ministry, and how His kingdom has been advanced through the game of baseball. Each of the men who work full time with UPI got the call to play professional baseball, was released from baseball, and was called up and *released* to follow God into this ministry.

Often I have asked why God would call me. What qualifications did I have? What did I know about ministry? I was just a guy from a small town who had been released from pro baseball.

I was the oldest of eight kids–Tom, Tim, Teri, Tracy, Todd, Tammy, Trudy, and Tony. We lived in a small house and shared one bathroom! We also shared great childhood memories. My dad is a man of integrity and hard work. He labored his entire life in the auto parts industry, and I don't remember his ever missing a day of work. My mom is positive and caring, and she sacrificed a lot for our family. When I was in high school, she took a third-shift job, working in an old stone woolen mill down by the Milwaukee River. After she had put all eight of us to bed, she would leave for work and return home just in time to see us off to school. During the day she often cared for other children. I wonder when she slept.

Every night we crowded around the table in our tiny kitchen for dinner. Now that all eight of us are adults, we have laughed about the names of some of my mom's meals: shipwreck, mix-mox, birds and dumplings—but we loved them all. We had plenty of food, a great yard for sports, and an Edsel station wagon. What more does a kid need? I was blessed with a great childhood.

My first eight years of school were at St. Joseph's, a private school, which was a sacrifice for my parents. They wanted the best for me, which meant an education with a moral foundation. I was not a great student—maybe it was because I had baseball on the brain. That preoccupation with baseball started in the fifth grade when I bought my first pack of baseball cards. They were a nickel a pack, and packs had four or five cards of unknown players along with a powdery piece of pink gum that was as stiff as the baseball cards. My friends and I traded cards to collect the players we wanted. We used the cards we didn't want for BB gun targets or we put them in our bicycle wheel spokes to make motorcycle sounds. Those crazy cards launched my love of the game.

Although I loved reading about and watching sports, involvement in athletics was not a part of my early childhood. I was too skinny and weak to be an athlete. But my love of baseball began to increase by listening to games on the radio. I became a fan of the Milwaukee Braves. My summer days after that consisted of wiffle ball in our side yard and hoops at our neighbor's house. In the winter we played baseball in the snow. In addition to baseball, a neighbor kid had a basketball hoop in his backyard. He was about my size, and we spent hours shooting hoops at his house.

Then one day I discovered the Green Bay Packers. They were playing in the 1960 NFL championship game against the Philadelphia Eagles. For some reason, I was drawn to that game. The Packers lost and my heart sank. I was hooked and after that my repertoire included football in the front yard. To this day I love the Packers.

My eighth grade teacher was a nun who was a huge New York Yankees fan. In those days, the Yanks were always in the playoffs, if not the World Series. I remember her closing the blinds in our cement block classroom, locking the door, and turning on an oversized black and white TV. We could choose either to read or watch the Yankees. Guess which option I chose? Thank you, Sister, wherever you are. You were the best.

By my freshman year in high school my focus was athletics. I had grown quite a bit over the summer, reaching 6'3" and weighing in at a whopping 122 pounds. Because of my height, the freshmen basketball coach took a chance on me and put me on his team. Although I never played, I made the team and practiced hard.

The sport I loved best, however, was still baseball. When the tryouts were announced my freshman year, I showed up and literally begged the coach for a spot on the team. High school baseball was played in the summertime in Wisconsin because of the short, cold, wet spring. For some reason, Coach Shultz allowed me to be on the team. There was only one uniform left, and it was three sizes too big, but I was proud to wear it. I was the guy who sat in the front of the bus and dreamed of being a star, but I never played. In Little League my position had been catcher, but with my size the coach thought I should pitch. I never took the mound that year, but I was happy just to be on the team.

By the time I graduated from high school I was fortunate to have played with some very good athletes and had collected a few honors. In my junior year our basketball team went to the state finals, and in my senior year our team was ranked in the top three all year. I led the league in scoring and began to hear from college basketball coaches. But my first love was still baseball.

By my senior year I opted out of playing summer baseball for the high school team and played instead in the Langsdorf League in Milwaukee. It was a very competitive semi-pro league with many big-name college players. It was a real challenge for me to pitch at that level, but I dreamed of playing pro ball so I needed to be stretched.

At the beginning of the season I did not experience much success. In fact, I think my record was something like 3 and 11. Then something happened. I was warming up for a night game and told my catcher that I couldn't really feel my arm and had no idea where the ball was going to go. His response was, "What's new?" As I took the mound that night, I had no idea that I was about to pitch at a whole new level. It all came together that night and my life was about to change. When the nine-inning game ended, we had upset the favored team, and I had struck out 18 hitters! It was a new league record.

To my surprise, there were two pro scouts in the grandstands. One was from the New York Mets and the other from the San Francisco Giants. They had come to scout another player, but after the game, Jack West of the San Francisco Giants stopped by the dugout and gave me his card. He said, "Remember kid, I was the first one to talk to you." Remember? How could I ever forget?

That was the beginning of a dream summer for a kid who loved baseball, and whose dream was to pitch in the big leagues. Scouts were calling the house and showing up at every game. Thirteen scouts had contacted me, and by July I had signed a bonus contract with the San Francisco Giants. I was assigned to Decatur, Illinois, of the Midwest league. My dream was coming true.

I vividly remember the day I left Milwaukee for spring training. The girl I was dating came with me to the airport and brought a gift. I was thinking it would be something pretty great since I had given her my Oldsmobile. It was a Bible. It even had my name engraved on the cover, so there was no way to "lose" it. Since I had already checked my luggage, I was stuck carrying *a Bible* onto the plane. It accompanied me on the long trip from Milwaukee to Phoenix to my spring training room in Casa Grande, Arizona. I thought then that maybe I would be able to hide it. But my first day in spring training I woke up to find the three other guys in my room having a Bible study. They may have been the only Christians in pro baseball at the time, and I ended up in their room. I carried my new Bible to the shower with me, hoping those guys would leave me alone, with no idea how much that book would change my life.

I would love to write about my successful baseball career. The reality was that my time with the Giants organization ended quickly. In the spring of 1968 Jack Schwartz, the general manager, called me into his office to tell me I was going home. That last trip to the locker room was tough. I had dreamed about the big career. I had imagined myself being able to take care of my parents who had sacrificed so much for me. My dream was dying, my world was crumbling, and my future looked empty. I had been released!

I found a phone booth, shut myself inside, and cried. I felt like a complete failure. What would my parents say? How could I face my friends who had sent me off as a hero? Would my girlfriend still want to go out with me? I called my parents to tell them I was coming home. At that moment I had no clue that God was going to use those experiences to bring me to Himself and prepare me for something bigger than my dreams.

On the flight home from Phoenix I thought about the conversation with my girlfriend in the car on our first date. She had shared the gospel with me, and all of a sudden it had more credibility. After a long lonely flight home, I landed in Milwaukee, wondering if anyone would be there. Both my parents and my girlfriend showed up. My parents were very kind and understanding. After all, I was their son, and they would love me whether I succeeded or not. But what about my girl? Would she still care about me? And what was I going to do with the rest of my life?

After returning home I took a few odd jobs, working first in a factory and then an aluminum foundry. At nights I hurried home to see my girlfriend. Yes, we continued to date. But it seemed like we went to church and Bible studies as much as to dinner and a movie. God was pursuing me. At the time I believed in God and went to church occasionally. I remember feeling sorry for Jesus for the way He had suffered. I thought I was a pretty good person.

One night my girlfriend's father took me to a sports banquet in Milwaukee. The speaker was Carroll Dale of the Green Bay Packers. I do not remember what he said, but I do remember that he was not ashamed to talk about his faith in Christ. I also remember thinking that his career as a pro athlete gave credibility to what he was saying. When a pro athlete speaks, people listen.

Several months after my release from baseball, my girlfriend asked if I had ever asked Jesus to personally come into my life. I told her I believed in Jesus. She explained that she meant asking Jesus to totally take over my life. I thought about that. It really made sense to me. I prayed a simple prayer, asking Jesus Christ to forgive my sins and take control of my life. I accepted His gift of salvation, knowing He was the Son of God and the only way to heaven. I really meant it. From that point on I had a personal faith in a personal God. It was not an emotional decision. I knew this eternity thing was something that had to be taken care of. It was the right thing to do. But my girlfriend knew my life would never be the same. That same night we went to visit Bryan and Del Coupland, the young couple who taught the Bible study we had attended. They spent several hours answering my questions and encouraging me in my faith. It was the beginning of a lifelong journey.

The issue of where I would spend eternity was resolved, but I still needed to think about a new career. God was already preparing the plan. He was opening a way for me to get into a new environment with new people. I had used part of my signing bonus to enroll at Career Academy to study radio and television broadcasting. As graduation approached, I sent out resumes to radio stations across America. I was intrigued that there were towns named Grafton in other states, so I sent a resume to stations in each of the Graftons. Why not? It would be easy to remember the name of the city from which we were broadcasting.

The West Virginia station responded immediately. I sent an audition tape, and within two months I was hired by station WVVW in Grafton, West Virginia. A friend and I boarded a plane in Milwaukee and flew to Pittsburgh. From there we hitchhiked to Grafton, West Virginia. We rented a place above a paint store for $8 a week, and my career in radio began.

WVVW was a typical small-town radio station in the 60s, playing a variety of music. The first day at the station was a Sunday. I was the rookie assigned the least desirable hours, and my job was to open the station at 6 a.m. The first radio show of the day featured Rev. Paul Moeller, a local pastor who preached live over the radio. I listened intently to what he had to say. When his half-hour program was over I said to him, "I think I believe what you believe."

That was the beginning of a very special relationship with the Moellers. Most evenings I would either play basketball for the church team or spend time in the Moellers' home. Mrs. Moeller fed me great homemade meals, and Pastor Moeller fed me God's Word. God had led me to this small coal town in West Virginia to plant His Word deep in my heart.

Some local colleges began to inquire about my playing basketball for them, and Rev. Moeller encouraged me to consider Grace College in Winona Lake, Indiana. He had attended Grace Seminary and thought Winona Lake was the place for me. I began to think about how much fun it might be to play small college basketball and get a Christian education at the same time. I decided to make the trip to Indiana to try out.

Coach Chet Kammerer was interested, but it didn't take long to discover that I was not eligible. At the time the N.A.I.A (National Association of Intercollegiate Athletics) did not allow anyone who had played professionally to compete at the college level in any sport. Since then the rules have changed. However, Coach Kammerer thought I could help both the basketball and baseball teams as a student coach/manager. It would help pay the tuition. So the following fall I enrolled as a freshman at Grace College.

While I was working my first year at the station in Grafton, West Virginia, my girlfriend came for a visit during the holidays. On New Year's Eve of 1969 I proposed, and on August 29, 1970, we were married. We moved everything we owned, which consisted of one dresser, an ancient sofa bed, and our wedding gifts to Winona Lake to begin our life together. A week after the wedding, we were living off campus as married students. I became a full-time student with various part time jobs, and Carin worked full time.

A few weeks before I graduated from Grace College with a B.S. degree in physical education and a minor in speech and drama, I was offered a teaching job in the Tippecanoe Valley school system in Indiana. For three years I taught speech and drama, coached varsity baseball and was the offensive coordinator for the football team. During that time our first daughter, Amy, was born on June 9, 1975. Hospitals were just beginning to allow fathers into the delivery room, and from the moment Amy entered the world, she locked her gaze on me and we bonded. I was full of love for her and, as they say, "She had me at first glance."

In 1979 I took a job at Huntington College in the admissions office and became the pitching coach for the baseball team. It was a great experience to work under head coach Jim Wilson. On June 26, 1979, our second daughter, Lindsay, arrived. We called her "Special K" because she has always been a special kid. Carin and I are blessed to have two wonderful girls in our lives. I have often been asked if I regretted not having a son. I can honestly say that I have never felt disappointed. Our daughters have taught me so much, and I love them a bunch.

In our third year at Huntington, Dr. John Davis, then president of Grace College, asked me to return to Grace as the head baseball coach. After much prayer I accepted, and Carin and I moved back to the Warsaw area. The three years as head coach gave me headaches, heartaches, wins, losses, and a great kick in the "grow up and get organized" part of the body. What a wonderful time.

At the time our pastor was Rev. Ivan French, an apostle Paul-type teacher. I tried never to miss church. Sitting under his teaching planted in me a desire to study and understand Scripture as he did. During that time we attended a missions conference at church, where the speaker's topic was "Reach the world." As I listened, the Holy Spirit spoke clearly to my heart. I was hit with the statement: "Tom, just reach *your* world."

That was a life-changing concept to me. I knew of missionaries going through training to learn a language and a culture so they could reach a certain people group. But the challenge now became personal. God was asking me to reach *my* world. I already spoke the language and knew the culture of a people group—*baseball players.* God was bringing all my past experiences together and pointing me in a new direction. Before I left the meeting that night, I had a long talk with God. I was now committed to using my baseball background for Him. But how? Wasn't I already doing that as a coach at a Christian college? Who could I talk with about this new direction?

It's Great to be alive because God is in control!

Action Points

- Have you ever written out your testimony?
- Take some time now to discuss what your life was like before coming to faith in Christ, how you came to believe in Him, and how your life has changed since then.

Play Ball

God had called me to reach my world, the world of baseball, for Him. I desired to use baseball as a vehicle for sharing Christ, but I didn't know how to begin. Then God began to open doors.

Our first evangelistic baseball clinic was held in Milwaukee the summer of 1979. The Billy Graham Association was holding a crusade in the city, and they were adding a free baseball clinic for kids. There was excitement in Milwaukee about the Brewers—professional baseball was back in town! A few years earlier, the Braves had moved to Atlanta and left a hole in the hearts of baseball-loving Wisconsin fans. The clinic was to be held at Martin Luther King Field, and Christian players from both the Brewers and the visiting Yankees were invited to attend.

Dave Kloke, a good friend from high school, called to tell me about the upcoming clinic. I was excited about the idea of sharing Christ in a baseball setting—and in my home area. I called the Graham offices to ask if I could be of any help, and they told me they had never run a baseball clinic. After a few phone calls and a personal meeting, I found myself in the grandstands of Milwaukee County Stadium writing a clinic format on a napkin. I don't remember much about the game that day, but that clinic format would end up serving UPI well for many years.

The day of the clinic about 300 kids showed up to hear Brewers' pitcher Bobby Galasso and Yankee players Tommy John, Brian Doyle, and Ray Burris. At the end of the baseball instruction, the players spoke with the kids about their faith.

Jerry Mullaney, reporter for *The Christian Courier* newspaper, wrote,

> About 75 youngsters came forward that day and were given counseling by several members of the Crusade Youth Committee. …Tom hopes to hold another such clinic here in Milwaukee next year…He has asked for our prayers in regard to the future of these clinics, insisting that "this whole thing has to be prayed through before we really start to take action. It may sound like pie in the sky, but our prayer life is always the bottom line. That's where it all begins." Simply by being available, these men were able to point beyond themselves toward that which is really important in life. It is certain that this kind of availability must be duplicated if we expect to change the world in the 1980's.

The clinic seemed to be a success, and the players enjoyed the time of sharing both baseball and Jesus. God was challenging me to step it up and live "sold out" for Him.

The next year UPI conducted another baseball clinic in Milwaukee, this time without the Graham Association or local churches. That was a learning experience. To conduct these clinics in a God-honoring way, we learned we needed other believers praying, helping with details, and following up with those who responded to the message.

The incident I recall most clearly about that outreach involved New York Yankees star pitcher Tommy John. He had agreed to help with the clinic along with two other players. The morning of the clinic I arrived at the hotel to pick up the three players who had agreed to do the outreach. There were only two in the lobby—Tommy John was nowhere to be found

What a disappointment it was as we drove to the ball field and wondered how the clinic would go without one of the star athletes. We discussed the clinic format with the other two players, and when we arrived at the field, we got to work. As we were signing in campers, creating teaching stations, and handing out equipment, Tommy John showed up.

Tom Meyers, Univ. of Wisconsin coach; Bob Watson, Brian Doyle, Tommy John, Tom Roy

Tommy's parents had made a surprise trip to Milwaukee to see their son. They arrived early that morning at the hotel and wanted to take him to breakfast. They went to a restaurant outside the team hotel, and when Tommy returned we had already left. He called a cab and paid his own way to the event. His word was his word, and that kind of integrity really spoke to me.

The clinic went well. More than three hundred kids attended, and the testimonies were clear. About 75 kids responded to the invitation to speak with counselors about a relationship with Christ. It was a learning experience, but we left feeling pretty good about the event. I felt I had given God a "tithe" of my time and talent and went back to my college job, thinking I had done what I was supposed to do. But God wasn't finished.

In November of 1979 I had received a call from Hal Jeffries. Hal was chaplain to the NFL Tampa Bay Buccaneers football team. He also worked closely with an organization called PAO (Pro Athletes Outreach), a leadership ministry to pro players from all sports. Through his contacts with PAO, Hal had secured the players for the clinic in Milwaukee. He was going to be in Chicago with the Bucs who were playing the Chicago Bears, so he called to see if we could meet him for lunch at the team hotel. Carin and I drove to Chicago along with our friends, Steve and Alice Petty.

We had a great time with Hal. We talked about the clinics in Milwaukee and that I hoped they could be yearly events. We talked about the summer business Steve Petty and I had started called Diamond Enterprises. We ran three-day baseball camps for local Little Leagues players, using the best high school coaches in the Midwest as instructors. The cost for three days was $19, and a portion went back to the kids leagues. This gave some revenue to the leagues, summer income to high school coaches, and provided good baseball instruction for the kids. It also provided a little extra income for us, which was much appreciated since we were living on a Christian college salary. At the time I had no idea that Diamond Enterprises was providing valuable training for UPI.

Hal listened with interest during the conversation. Then he dropped a bombshell! He turned to me after the meal, looked me right in the eye, and said something like this: "When are you going to quit doing nickel and dime stuff for God and step out on faith and do what God has made you for?" Talk about a 100 mph fastball right at my head. I didn't know what to say. Wasn't working for a Christian college enough?

In my best Christian tone I told Hal I would "pray about it." It was an uncomfortable moment for me. I couldn't get what Hal had said out of my mind. On the two-hour drive back to Indiana we were chewing on what direction God wanted us to take. Alice Petty suggested that maybe Diamond Enterprises should turn into a full-time Christian outreach.

Not long after that, I received a call from Dave Swanson, a good friend of Hal's and the executive director of Baseball Chapel. Baseball Chapel had been started in the early '60s to provide chapel services for every team in professional baseball. There were some great men involved in starting Baseball Chapel, including Waddy Spoelstra, Sam Bender, Bobby Richardson, and Al Worthington.

Dave was located in New York City and needed someone to serve as chaplain for the Nets, Jets, and Mets. He asked if I would be interested in interviewing for the position. (I'm guessing Hal Jeffries gave him a call.) It was pretty exciting to go to New York and meet with him. Maybe God was leading me to work with three of the pro teams in the "Big Apple."

Dave asked very pointed questions about my family, my theology, and my giftedness. He listened intently to the answers. I felt good about the meeting and thought I had nailed it. However, in a way only Dave could, he told me I was not the right man for the job. I was stunned. We were willing to move to the big city to take on this huge job, and now he was telling me I was not right for the job. Then he told me this job with the Nets, Jets, and Mets was too small for me. He told me with my evangelistic gift I needed to be sharing Jesus with the world, not just New York City.

As nice as that sounded, I left that meeting feeling defeated. I had given it my best shot and did not get the job. My pride was wounded. I didn't understand at the time that God was speaking to me through Dave. Thank you, Dave Swanson, for being God's man of the hour. I will always be grateful. Dave continued to serve with Baseball Chapel for many years before he passed away in 2001.

So, where did that leave us? I was enjoying the coaching but still thinking that God had a different plan for me. My dream to this point was to be a successful college coach. I would have been very happy to always be known as "coach." But the idea of a baseball ministry would not leave me.

Some time later Hal Jefferies took me to a PAO baseball conference. He wanted to show me that there were quite a few baseball players who loved Jesus. It was an eye opener. The conference provided great teaching, plus one-on-one time with professional baseball players and their wives. There were players who could share their faith. Arlis Priest, the founder of PAO, and Norm Evans, the president of PAO, showed genuine interest and encouraged us in the direction I felt God was leading. PAO was very instrumental in what would happen next.

One day I made an appointment with Mike Valentine, a local attorney, who 20 years later would become one of my closest friends. As I shared my dream with him, he listened carefully and asked strategic questions. When the meeting was over, he was encouraging and said he would begin drawing up the government paperwork. We discussed cost, and he gave me a figure. We set up a monthly payment schedule.

On December 22, 1980, I got a call from his office, informing me that UPI had been granted 501(c)(3) not-for-profit status. I hurried down to the law office to sign the paperwork. I remember right before signing on the dotted line, he stopped me and said to think it through carefully. He reminded me that once the papers were signed, I would be known publicly as the leader of a Christian organization. There would be no hiding that fact from the government or anyone else. I thought about it deeply for about 10 seconds and signed the papers.

After the last payment was made for incorporation, Mike handed me a check for the full amount of the payments. It was the first gift to UPI and a huge encouragement to me that God was in this work. We were about to begin publicly sharing the gospel of Jesus Christ through the game of baseball.

By-laws and Articles of Incorporation for UPI

The objects of the association shall be: any and all lawful purposes consistent with the provisions of I.C.23-7-1, to I.C. 23-7-1.1.66 and in particular the purpose of glorifying God through the spreading of His good news, the Gospel, to youth and adults.

The major emphasis of this ministry will be the administration of evangelistic baseball clinics in major league cities. Ballplayers and coaches will share their testimonies, and an invitation will be given for those in attendance to accept Jesus Christ as their personal Savior.

From the beginning, God was showing us that this was a ministry that would reach into Major League baseball for the purpose of sharing the gospel in a unique venue. Now that UPI was a legitimate organization, what came next? Should I continue coaching? How would I make a living? Would we be able to get players involved? Were there enough big league guys that loved Jesus who would embrace this new ministry? How would other ministries feel about this new baseball ministry?

It's Great to be alive because God is in control!

Action Point

- Describe some divine appointments that God has put in your life.

It's Official

With the paperwork completed, UPI was a legitimate ministry in the eyes of the government. The first office was in the basement of our home with a card table, a folding chair, and a brown rotary telephone. Shortly after beginning the ministry, Wisconsin businessman Ed Taylor generously donated a desk, bookshelves, and other office materials. I spent those early days in the office on the phone, making contacts and out on the road, visiting with others in the sports ministry field. Men like Jack King of Athletes in Action and Sam Bender of Baseball Chapel were very positive and encouraging to me in those early years. During that time I was also in contact with a number of churches and pastors for the purpose of sharing the vision of UPI whenever possible.

UPI was not a full-time venture in 1981. For the first three years of the ministry, I worked for Grace College during the school year and spent summers in ministry, conducting baseball clinics and speaking at chapels for major league baseball teams. Sam Bender made me an itinerant chaplain for the Midwest teams. He would call early each spring to ask which chapel services I would like to do. I was often in a different city each Sunday as a chapel speaker. The typical rotation was Milwaukee, Cincinnati, Detroit, Pittsburgh, Cleveland, and the two Chicago teams. Chapels were usually held in the locker room and attendance fluctuated from 5 to 25. What a great opportunity! God was allowing me to develop relationships with current players. Many of those men would later volunteer for UPI clinic outreaches and mission trips.

At that time I was the executive director of UPI, a ministry of one, with Steve Petty an acting advisor. Our first business was to form a board of directors. The first recorded minutes of a board meeting were from February 9, 1981. The UPI minutes from that first meeting recorded a balance of $294.19 and $700 in outstanding bills.

I was the first chairman of the board, simply because I was the only one who knew what was going on. Within a short time the board had appointed a new chairman. One of the first orders of business in that February meeting was to create our outreach strategy for churches sponsoring UPI clinics. We put together a packet of information on how to organize a clinic and form the necessary committees. The packet included follow-up letters, sample press releases, and the financial responsibilities of the church and UPI. This packet was used for many years.

The first official board of UPI consisted of the following men in addition to myself:

- Hal Jeffries, chaplain to the Tampa Bay Buccaneers football team
- Kent Fishel, director of Discipleship Incorporated
- Jim Wilson, businessman and former head baseball coach at Huntington College
- Al Buhler, director of the local Child Evangelism Fellowship
- Larry Poyser, a local insurance agent and a trustee at his church
- Later that year, local businessman Bill Bufton was added to the board.

The men who came alongside UPI in the beginning stages were fundamental in forming the direction and philosophy of the ministry. Since that time I have told many men who were starting a new work to form a board of godly men for guidance, accountability, and prayer.

The first official UPI baseball camp for kids was held in North Webster, Indiana, the summer of 1981. The camp lasted for a week and just over 30 kids attended. The purpose of the camp was to teach kids the fundamentals of the game as well as to build Christ into their lives. During that year God also provided a number of speaking engagements at churches and athletic banquets. It was a great time for gaining experience in public speaking and for learning to give my testimony. God was preparing me for the future.

We were geared up for a summer of baseball clinics in 1981 when Major League Baseball went on strike. What a discouraging start for a young ministry. There would be no major league baseball for clinics that first year.

In the early years of the ministry I felt like a one-man show, responsible for every detail. I learned the importance of having a good understanding of one's gifts and passions. I love being the guy who blazes the path, but I knew I needed others around me with different gifts. One pressing need at UPI was for someone with financial skills. God answered that need with the addition of Phil Menzie to the board in February of 1982.

Phil was a controller for a local company, and with his accounting skills he made a great addition to the board as treasurer. Shortly after taking the board position, Phil became UPI's first administrator. He took the burden of all the financial details off my shoulders. I was a coach, learning to be a minister. God had provided a man with the gifts UPI needed and the timing was perfect.

Phil also helped with conducting clinics and contacting players. One of his favorite memories was a clinic scheduled for a Saturday morning in Cincinnati. The game on Friday night endured five rain delays and finally ended around 1:30 a.m. But Dave Roberts of the Phillies had promised to help with the clinic, and he did. He was the only pro player who showed up. It was a sacrifice on his part to give up precious hours of sleep to attend the clinic. It was another early sign to us that God was going to provide.

During the winter months I continued to work at Grace College. Finances were not sufficient for full-time ministry. In an effort to raise funds and share the vision of UPI, we decided to hold a special banquet in the spring of 1982 to introduce local people to UPI. Other ministries conducted fundraising banquets and encouraged us to try the same approach. Hal Jeffries was the speaker along with three Chicago Bears football players: linebacker Brian Cabral,

Banquet speakers: Hall Jeffrey, Tom Roy, Brian Cabral, Mike Cobb, Vince Evans

quarterback Vince Evans, and tight end Mike Cobb. Those football players drew a capacity crowd and did a great job. The evening included a sports memorabilia auction, but the event brought in only $680. We had serious questions about whether this was the way we were supposed to raise support. It was a lot of work for minimal results, but at least the word was getting out.

Faith Bible Church of Milwaukee sponsored the first clinic in June of 1982 with help from other area churches. UPI clinics are usually conducted on a Saturday morning in a big league city. UPI secures the athletes from both the home team and visiting team and provides free baseball instruction. Local churches train counselors, secure a field and pay the bills. Pastor Terry Angles and Lee Luckman did an outstanding job of coordinating the outreach and more than 1,100 kids and their parents attended. Milwaukee Brewers Paul Molitor, Marshall Edwards, Ned Yost, Bob McClure, Jim Gantner, Mark Brouhard, and Jerry Augustine gave instruction in baseball along with

Detroit Tigers John Wokenfuss, Dave Tobik, Bill Fahey, and Hall of Fame announcer Ernie Harwell. At the end of the clinic several of the players shared their life story, and I gave the gospel. More than 120 indicated they wanted Jesus in their lives. Terry Angles and his committee had trained 75 counselors to follow up with those who responded. They had planned well and worked hard, and God gave them great results. UPI is indebted to Terry and his church for taking the risk of believing in UPI in the early days and then working hard to make the outreaches happen.

Here are some letters from that outreach:

Dear Tom, I was very happy to be part of a very successful Milwaukee clinic. Thanks again and may God bless you and Unlimited Potential Inc. A friend always, Jim Gantner.

…Let's all hope and pray that someday we can have a similar outreach service in the Detroit area. Ernie Harwell, announcer, Detroit Tigers.

Dear Tom, I really enjoyed doing the clinic. God gave me baseball gifts, and if I can bring people closer to Jesus Christ, then I'm happy. Keep up the good work. You are doing a great job. Ned Yost, catcher, Milwaukee Brewers.

In July of 1982 we conducted our second USA baseball outreach in Akron, Ohio. The sponsoring church was The Chapel in University Park with pastor David Burnham. Bob Provost was given the job of coordinating the clinic, and he was a great encouragement to me as a new minister.

Because of rain, we were forced to move the clinic indoors to Firestone Gymnasium, which was a first. It was another learning experience. How do you hold a baseball clinic for more than a thousand kids if it rains? In spite of the bad weather, an estimated crowd of 1,650 showed up. Instructors included Rick Waits, Mike Hargrove, and John Denny of the Indians, and Barry Foote of the New York Yankees.

Pastor Paul Gerdes, who was responsible for organizing the on-field portion of the clinic, said:

I know that you had a good overall plan and that a number of people worked very hard, but I believe the tremendous attendance on such a rotten day was a demonstration of God's blessing in support of the ministry. I am grateful for you and the interaction that we have been able to have in working together for this ministry. I'm looking forward to times of fellowship and labor in the future.

The following is from one of the adults who brought a group with him:

Dear Tom, I appreciated very much being at the baseball clinic in Cleveland, and my seven guys were really excited about it. Two boys responded to the invitation. I will be watching them closely as to just what this meant to them. Most Cordially, Ken Anderson, Ken Anderson Films.

Later that summer, after a few weeks of speaking in churches and conducting a baseball camp at Grace College, I boarded a plane to Oliver, British Columbia, to participate in the Okanagan Major League Baseball Camp. Don Coy and Dale Parker were co-owners of the camp and both were Christian men, and they wanted a Christian influence. I was to be the pitching coach and lead devotions at night. What a great opportunity! Many young men gave their lives to Christ at that camp, including one named Tim Dell.

As the clinic year ended, the board minutes recorded, "Tom has done this for two years for free. At the conclusion of the summer or earlier if possible, the board will pay the director an honorarium in proportion to the amount of funds received." I cannot remember the amount, but I am confident the board was generous.

I continued to work for Ron Henry as assistant director of admissions at Grace College. Ron was a great boss and friend and could see my love for baseball ministry. He knew that God was working in a special way in my life. Part of my job description at Grace was to be an international student recruiter, which meant I would travel to missionary schools around the world to share the ministry of Grace College and Theological Seminary. The college allowed me, even encouraged me, to combine recruiting travel with ministry opportunities overseas. Carin and I will always be grateful to the college and to Ron Henry for their support, and for graciously allowing me to work part time as the ministry of UPI was getting off the ground.

I attended a youth conference in Harvey Cedars, New Jersey, as a Grace College representative. There I met Dave Pollack, the founder of Interaction, Inc., a ministry to missionary kids. Dave traveled overseas, visiting many missionary and international schools. He took me on many trips with him and became a mentor to me. I visited those schools to represent Grace College, but God used the trips to expand my worldview. My eyes were opened wide to the need for Jesus all around the globe. My vision for UPI began to expand to include taking pro players on international trips. I asked God to use that vision however He saw fit.

In 1982 we had our first church jump on board financially. Carin and I attended Pleasant View Bible Church, which was a very missions-minded congregation. They decided to take on UPI with monthly support. We were very encouraged and humbled by this support and by the many who faithfully prayed for this new ministry.

1982 was also the year I met Norm Wilhelmi, the man God used to start the National Christian College Athletic Association (NCCAA). He had his own Christian sports radio spot, and he conducted a preseason baseball tournament for Christian college teams in Florida. Norm is a real entrepreneur. I took the Grace College baseball team to play in that tournament and Norm and I hit it off. That was the beginning of a great friendship. In 1983 Norm asked me to return to help him, and eventually he made me his assistant in the venture. My role was to be tournament chaplain, bringing in

Norm Wilhelmi

current pro players to share with the students one night a week. That spring Christian College tournament would enable many young people to hear the gospel, and we continue to work with Norm to this day.

There is something to be said for those individuals who believe in a vision with such conviction that they risk failure. People like Dave Pollack, Norm Wilhelmi, and the folks at Pleasant View Bible Church had tremendous influence in my life and in the ministry of UPI. They believed in what God was doing through us and they encouraged us.

On one occasion Tom Randall, pioneer missionary to the Philippines, told me, "I really think your work with the players is a way to go and a very fruitful ministry. I pray you can continue to make contacts and disciple more of those guys for the kingdom."

In November of 1982 we did a second banquet. Things were moving fast, and we needed to raise funds. The banquet cost $1,721.75 and brought in $1,699. The auction brought in $322. About $4,000 in pledges were made, but much of that never came in. It was becoming clear that UPI was not going to raise funds through banquets.

In December Paul Refior joined our board. Paul is a local attorney who has a passion for ministry and winning souls for Christ. The records show that with Paul Refior on the board the ministry took on a larger worldview. Paul had a vision to expand and reach the entire world through baseball. He would eventually become the chairman, and he was uniquely used by God to move UPI to a new level.

It's Great to be alive because God is in control!

Action Points

- Have you ever come alongside anyone in a new ministry that needed someone to believe in him or her?

- Think through the first few years of your Christian life and recall the people God used to influence and encourage you.

The Game Plan

As the UPI board was taking shape, my vision and responsibilities were growing. I was being stretched, and it became obvious that we needed a mission statement to define our direction. So in December of 1982 Paul Refior, Phil Menzie, and I met with Jim Wilson to strategically plan for the future of UPI. Our meeting was held at picturesque Camp Pinnacle in the Helderberg Mountains in upstate New York, a perfect place to get away to seek God's direction.

After two days of meetings we drove to New Hampshire to meet with Dave Pollack of Interaction ministries. It was a valuable time for working through a vision for the future of UPI. In the beginning that vision consisted of baseball clinics for kids, conducted in partnership with local churches in the USA. But God was expanding that vision to reach beyond US borders. Every house must have a builder. God had laid the foundation. Now He was slowly showing us a blueprint for ministry.

The first UPI international trip was to Puerto Rico. On Christmas day, 1982, our team gathered at a hotel near Chicago's O'Hare airport. Going from the blustery cold winds of Chicago to the smells of freshly cut grass and warm ocean breezes was in itself worth the trip. The team of men who joined me on this trip included Jake Boss, a high school coach from Lansing, Michigan; Andy Hill, assistant professor of biblical studies and assistant baseball coach at Trinity International University in Deerfield, Illinois; and Al Strong, a former Grace College baseball player. We were excited to serve Christ through baseball and to see the opportunities on this beautiful island. We also were excited to escape the winter weather in the Midwest.

Baseball clinic in Puerto Rico

Puerto Rico is a baseball paradise. During the winter, many professional players from the States are in Puerto Rico to play in the winter leagues. We found a number of those players who were interested in helping us with the clinics, men like Chris Bando and Edwin Aponte. Later Chris became a UPI associate.

After that trip Andy Hill wrote, "It's exciting to view Christians in other parts of the world…the people were eager for UPI to return…Need to pray for more Spanish-speaking pros for the future." How true that statement was then and still is today.

Plan to Win

UPI was in a "plan to win" mode. We knew that to see sustained growth, we needed to better define the responsibilities that were necessary for the ministry to flourish. Here is a copy of the first job description for the Director of Unlimited Potential:

> The Director of Unlimited Potential shall oversee the direction and management of the work of Unlimited Potential Incorporated.

UPI's first international team. Pictured are Puerto Rican pastor and friends with Tom Roy (center), Al Strong, Dr. Andrew Hill, and Jake Boss.

Included in those jobs will be the responsibility to:

- Contact local pastors for the purpose of setting up clinics in major league cities
- Visit churches involved in the outreaches
- Oversee the contact with professional baseball players
- Set up and maintain the major league baseball prayer line
- Visit players in spring training facilities
- Maintain contacts through letters and phone calls with professional athletes
- Contact foreign mission boards and churches overseas for the implementation of international outreach
- Visit international outreach cities prior to clinics
- Be responsible for leadership, devotions, and maintenance of overseas operations during outreach

- Handle finances as relates to the cost of each participant in overseas ministry
- Choose the team to represent UPI, as well as delegate responsibilities once on the field. Maintain contact with missionaries and pro players after outreach for the purpose of encouragement and to stress the importance of good follow-up programs
- Oversee the direction of the Camping Division, and keep data as it relates to camping dates, coaches participating, finances, and attendance
- Instruct camps when needed
- Maintain contact with camping director throughout the year
- Compile and send out college placement lists to those who are members of the National Christian College Athletic Association
- Represent Unlimited Potential at speaking engagements around the world, including churches, FCA groups, athletic teams, and Christian colleges, as well as professional baseball chapel services
- Be available for missions conferences and spiritual life weeks
- Serve on the board of directors, having one vote and reporting monthly to the board of directors on the activities of the previous month
- Share vision as well as concerns of the ministry with the board of directors

●

UPI was growing, and my responsibilities were increasing. Phil Menzie had joined UPI part time as an administrator to oversee the finances of the ministry and he began to assist with my responsibilities when I was on the road. In the spring of 1983, I had submitted my letter of resignation as the head baseball coach at Grace College, a tough decision as I truly loved the players. It was also time to step down from my position in the admissions office at Grace. Shortly after that, UPI board chairman Paul Refior sent a personal letter to about seventy people on our mailing list informing them of my intention to leave my position at Grace and begin working full time with UPI as of January 1, 1984. In that letter he mentioned the need for $40,000 to cover all the ministry expenses. We didn't know how God would meet that need, but we were committed.

By the summer of 1983 UPI was in full swing, even though I was still part-time. We had evangelistic baseball clinics scheduled in Cincinnati, Milwaukee, Akron, Philadelphia, Chicago, and Detroit. God was building His work. Here are some highlights from that summer:

- In Cincinnati, 19 people indicated they had placed faith in Jesus. Players helping with the outreach included Bob Knepper, Terry Puhl, and Craig Reynolds of the Houston Astros.

- Milwaukee had a huge turn out—more than 2,700 registered for the clinic! The Brewer players that participated were Paul Molitor, Jim Gantner, Robin Yount, Jerry Augustine, Don Sutton, Rob Picciolo, Sal Bando, and Chuck Porter. The Seattle Mariners in attendance were Dave Edler, Jamie Allen, and Bill Plummer. Pastor Terry Angles reported approximately 125 first-time decisions for Christ.

- In Philadelphia, more than 300 attended, and Mike Easler, Brian Harper, and Lee Tunnel of the Pittsburgh Pirates did the training and sharing.

- Chicago had 51 indicate a commitment to Jesus, and the players who came out to help included Scott Fletcher of the White Sox and Kenny Schrom and Dave Engle of the Twins.

- In Akron, Chris Bando and Juan Eichelberger of the Indians and Paul Molitor, Jim Gantner, and Chuck Porter of the Brewers addressed the more than 1,000 in attendance.

Tom Roy with players from Detroit Tigers and Cleveland Indians

- In Detroit, 400 showed up to hear Ernie Harwell and Bill Fahey of the Tigers as well as Wayne Gross and Bill Almon of the Oakland A's. Forty people indicated a first-time faith.

During that summer UPI conducted its second baseball camp, this time at Grace College. I was also the pitching coach again at the Okanagan Major League Baseball Camp in British Columbia. It was a full summer.

Later that year we made a second trip to Puerto Rico. There was an added dimension to the outreach this time. Puerto Rico is a U.S. territory, and, therefore, students were eligible for U.S. college grants. We began conducting tryouts for kids ages 16-20, evaluating the talent as well as sharing the gospel. We assisted those who showed ability to obtain scholarships to play college baseball in the U.S. at Christian colleges and universities. In the first two years, 10 players enrolled in Christian colleges to play baseball as a result of these tryouts. By the end of the decade nearly 125 Puerto Rican young people were attending Christian colleges, playing baseball, and growing in their relationship with Christ.

Before going into the ministry full time, we tried once again to raise the local exposure of UPI. Instead of a banquet, we held an auction of sports items donated by players. The auctioneer was local pastor Charles Ashman, and the speakers were Fritz Peterson, former pitcher for the New York Yankees and Van Crouch, the chaplain for the Chicago Bears and Cubs. Once again, we didn't raise much money, but we hope prayers were raised.

We were not doing too well in the fundraising department. The whole idea of asking for money made both Carin and me very uncomfortable. In a bold move for me, I decided to approach one of the Milwaukee Brewers to ask him to consider becoming involved with UPI financially. His answer was a gracious no. I hit my knees. My questions to God were from the heart. In a matter of months we were going to be in full-time ministry. How was this work going to be funded? Where would the money come from? How would we live?

Carin and I now faced an exciting, yet frightening, year ahead. It was time to step out full time with the work God was doing. I knew God was leading me in this direction. It was confirmed when the Spirit of God spoke to Carin's heart. We had been receiving a salary from Grace College. At the time the college was celebrating its 25th anniversary and rejoicing that God had provided for the school for 25 years. It hit her that we could continue to have faith in the college for our income, a college that existed by faith in God, or we could "go direct." In a newsletter written by Carin in October of 1983 she stated:

> God has graciously kept Tom remarkably healthy in spite of his hectic pace, even when exposed to unfriendly viruses by family and friends. I marvel at this because he has always been notorious for being the first to pick up the latest "bug." As his schedule grows more demanding, God's protection is increasingly evident. We praise Him for it and sincerely thank you for your prayers. Thank you also for praying for and encouraging the girls and me while Tom is away from home. It helps more than you know.
>
> We are eager to begin. This decision to step out full-time on faith, giving up a secure income, has been surrounded with much prayer and thoughtful consideration. We are confident this is the ministry God has designed for us (and us for it). We are certain that this is His timing. We can see His hand at work. Recently Tom commented that if he were a business-

man, it would have taken him many years to meet the people God has brought into our lives in the past year alone. We are very humbled, a little frightened, awed by the "unlimited potential" this ministry could have, but most of all—eager.

Carin has always been a strong support and an encouragement in this ministry. It became apparent to me later how important it is to have a supportive wife. She made it possible for me to travel for the ministry because she was willing to take care of things at home. As the time approached for us to be full time, we were excited about doing something no one else had done. But our biggest challenges were yet ahead. The transition to full-time ministry was a little bumpy. In another newsletter Carin wrote:

> Since our decision to be full-time with Unlimited Potential, we've been very aware of an enemy who would like to have us discouraged. In the past months we've sensed our commitment being tested in various ways, including Tom's ankle injury while in Okinawa. We've needed to spend many weeks apart in order to launch this young ministry, and it seems whenever Tom leaves, trouble strikes—broken water lines, frozen pipes, water damage, broken appliances, and car trouble. But we can already see that through each situation God can bring us to a better place.
>
> I am often asked "How do you handle having Tom gone so much?" The answer is that I don't always handle it well. But God is using this time to teach me some things. First, that I can't always handle it well, and I desperately need to draw from His strength. Second, I'm learning how valuable Christian friends are who support with prayer, encouragement, and action. Third, He's helping me use the time to improve in some areas like time-management and being organized. Fourth, He's teaching us both the importance of scheduling special family time together.

Another blow came to us in February. The outreach in Cleveland the prior summer had gone well, but a reporter from the *Cleveland Plain Dealer*, who had attended the clinic, was not impressed. He wrote a scathing article about how the ballplayers tried to trick kids into a faith in Jesus. This came as a blow to me. We had been careful to advertise, "players will be sharing their faith in Christ with an emphasis on commitment." We were concerned the article could damage the ministry as it was just getting started. Already, the Cleveland clinic for the following summer was on hold. But God used this for good, as the response to the article was overwhelming. In the following days, the letters to the editor were five to one in favor of the players sharing Jesus at the clinic. It was a serious bump in the road, but we moved on.

In February and March Phil Menzie and I traveled for the first time to spring training sites in Florida to encourage players and hold Bible studies for them. We also wanted to make them aware of what UPI had to offer. We met with players from the Yankees, Pirates, Phillies, Red Sox, White Sox, Mets, Tigers, and Astros. In those days we didn't have cell phones, text messaging, e-mail, or even faxes. We needed to go face-to-face. In an effort to have more "face time" with the players, I took the suggestion of a friend and had postcards printed with my picture on them. I used them for correspondence with players, and it worked. Often players would mention how they had seen me somewhere but couldn't remember where. In reality they had seen my face on a postcard.

In April and May my schedule really got crazy. Delta Airlines offered a special fare of $700 for 21 days of unlimited travel anywhere in the U.S. All I had to do was show up at the airport and board the plane. In those 21 days I traveled to Cleveland, Cincinnati, Philadelphia, New York, Chicago, Milwaukee, San Juan, Atlanta, Seattle, San Francisco, and Dallas. Usually I would meet with players during the day and fly coast to coast on a red eye flight, so I could sleep on the plane and not have to get a hotel room. In the morning I would shower in a locker room or at a player's apartment. In those days there were many short nights and a lot of fast food.

1984 Clinics:

- Milwaukee – 1,400 attended the clinic, seven Brewers and two Cleveland Indian players provided the instruction. Milwaukee would turn out to be an anchor location for UPI.

- Chicago - Pastor Bill Timm directed another great outreach and players Scott Fletcher of the White Sox and Oakland A's players Mike Davis, Bill Almon, and Bill Essian taught and shared. It was my first of many meetings with Mike Davis. He became a UPI regular for sharing and outreach in the years ahead.

- Philadelphia and Cincinnati also had outreaches, and new names were added to the growing list of major league players who volunteered, including Otis Nixon, Brett Butler, Jaime Kitchener, Bobby Clark, Larry Andersen, Kevin Bass, Duane Walker, and Tom Foley. God continued to give us favor with the players and the churches and was blessing UPI.

In July of 1984 Jake Boss became our first director of camps. Jake coached a high school team in Lansing, Michigan, and was not only an excellent instructor, but also very capable in sharing the gospel. Camps in 1984 included Camp Adventure in North Webster, Indiana, and the Okanagan camp in British Columbia. Another first for UPI was that Phil Menzie was given a whopping salary of $50 per month as administrator. It wasn't much, but it was a way to say thanks for his service. In November the board determined that the director's salary for 1985 would be $9,200. I was in the big bucks now!

Probably the most exciting event of that year happened in September when God opened a huge door of opportunity in Mainland China. Through the efforts of John Bechtel and Scott Hall, UPI was able to make direct contact with the China Sports Service Company in Los Angeles at the time of the 1984 Olympics. Vice Chairman Chen Chun Lai met with Paul Refior, and by the end of that meeting they had set dates, programs, and locations for UPI's first visit to China. Paul Refior wrote:

Baseball is played in only five provinces of China but is virtually unknown in many of the interior regions of the land. Amazingly, it is to these interior provinces (where Westerners and many missionaries cannot go) that this agency of the Communist government is enthusiastically inviting UPI to come.

This was all God's doing. By 1985 UPI would have boots on the ground in China.

To Thailand

At the end of 1984, our first full-time year, Harold Reynolds, all-star second baseman for the Seattle Mariners, made the long trip with me to Bangkok, Thailand, to conduct baseball clinics. British Airways gave us free first class tickets. Wow, baseball wasn't even a well-known sport in Britain. The trip was extra long. Our travel did not take us the most direct route through San Francisco or Seattle, but because we were on British Air, we went through London...the long way around the world.

Maybe you are wondering if they even know what baseball is in Thailand. We were invited by an American businessman living in Bangkok. He loved baseball and wanted to see the game promoted in Thailand. I responded to his request and told him of our Christian emphasis and wrote that we needed to have the backing of Christian churches and that the players would be sharing their faith in Jesus at the clinics. He loved baseball enough to get us letters from seven Christian churches of varied flavors to help with the outreaches. After much prayer and consideration, we made the trip.

Our adventures began before we reached Bangkok. We had an overnight layover in London. Harold said he had a high school friend who was living and working in the leather district of London and had offered us housing. This friend was a very tall female who showed up wearing a leather vest and a mini skirt over orange and white-striped leotards! I wasn't so sure about Harold's friend. He said she wasn't this "outgoing" when she was in high school. We went to lunch together and she literally "parted the sidewalk" as people turned to stare. I was wondering what we had gotten ourselves into.

It turned out she was also a dancer, and she invited us to go with her to an audition with a dance group at a nightclub called "Bananas." What would my friends back home think? But we had no choice, since we didn't know where she lived, and she was our housing for the evening. Bananas was a scene out of a Star Wars movie. There were young and old with an assortment of hair colors and body piercings. The place was packed and filled with smoke. The audition was not until after midnight, so we just sat and took in the sights of London.

It turned into a divine appointment as this young woman poured her heart out to us. We were able to give her some hope and direction. God astounded her, and when we left it was clear she was thinking seriously about Jesus.

After a brutal 24 hours of travel, Harold and I finally arrived in the land of Buddha. As soon as we landed we were rushed to a baseball field. There was a crowd of about 200 gathered at the International School of Bangkok to see the two of us show how the game of baseball was played. I put Harold in the field as I spoke to the crowd from the home plate area. Harold moved from position to position as I hit fly balls and ground balls to show how the game was played. By the time we had covered every position, Harold was gassed.

Following the demonstration there was a game between two American teams that had been assembled by the Bangkok Baseball Federation. Harold played for one of the teams, and I pitched for both. By the end of seven innings in the 95-degree heat, we were both ready for water and sleep.

Over the next ten days we held baseball clinics for all ages. It was great to get to know the people and have the opportunity to share Jesus at the end of each clinic. Many of the campers were Americans, but there were also children from Australia, Finland, Canada, and Thailand. Eyes were opened and hearts were touched by the message of Christ.

The trip proved to be a great bonding time for Harold and me. He had been willing to take a chance by going on a mission trip to Bangkok with a man he hardly knew. We spent many hours in Bible studies at the hotel and in the van on our way to the fields. Harold talked about this trip with his Seattle Mariners teammates during the following spring training. As a result of that trip, UPI would develop some life-long friendships with others on that team, like Mike Moore, Dave Valle, Alvin Davis, and Dave Edler. After a brilliant baseball career Harold Reynolds went on to become a well-recognized baseball announcer. I am grateful to Harold for taking a risk.

Tug Hullet, Jed Hansen, sponsors Deb & Bill Reinsch, and Tom Roy in Bangkok

UPI has made many trips to Thailand since then, and we have made some wonderful friends, including businessman Bill Reinsch and missionary Kelly Davidson and their families. We have also made some great memories. One story that sticks in my mind is the time a lovely young girl attended one of the clinics. She had beautiful skin and long, dark hair. Each of the pros on this trip commented on the striking 11 year old. We were all shocked to learn she was a guy. We learned he was a Sikh, and Sikh men do not cut their hair.

Even more surprising than finding out our camper was a boy, was watching how God worked in his life. As we conducted the clinic this young man noticed that each of us had on a bracelet. At the time, colorful "What Would Jesus Do" wristbands were becoming popular. The bracelets caught his attention because a Sikh is required to wear a gold bracelet to remind him of God. He asked me questions about the bracelet and wondered if he could have one.

I told him that the bracelet was a reminder to us that we are responsible before God for every decision we make. He liked that. Then I told him that I would be glad to give one to him if he would first read the entire New Testament. He said he was willing, but would have to ask his father's permission. I agreed he needed to do that. The next day he returned with the good news that his father had given him permission to read it. I was pumped. By the end of our time in Bangkok that year, he returned to tell me that he had read Matthew through Revelation. I asked him the obvious question: What did he think of Jesus? He responded that he was very interested in learning more and would read about Jesus again. I gave him my bracelet. I do not know if this young man came to faith, but I do know that "faith comes by hearing and hearing comes from the Word of God." (Romans 10:17) He now has the Word of God in him. God has unique ways to get His gospel out to the nations.

It's Great to be alive because God is in control!

Action Points

- Life is full of challenges, surprises, and setbacks. Have you ever found yourself in an uncomfortable situation? How did you handle it?

- What have you learned from setbacks?

- Have you ever recognized a surprise encounter as a divine appointment?

Unsung Heroes

Enthusiasm, expectation, and pain are meaningful words for those who call themselves Chicago Cubs fans.

Wherever you go, you can find Cubs fans, and you have to love and respect them for their loyalty. I have seen Cubs jerseys on the back roads of Uganda and even on the South Side of Chicago, a place where typically the black and white of the White Sox are the colors of choice. There is no doubt that the Cubs have many loyal fans. But with all the hoopla there have been very few pennants. And there have been few years the Cubs have had a playoff berth.

One of those years was 1998, and although it took a team effort, a little known backup outfielder became the unsung hero. After playing five years as the left fielder for the Milwaukee Brewers, Matt Meiske found himself on the bench as a backup outfielder for the Cubs. A lifetime .262 hitter, Matt became a trivia question after his pinch hit sent the Cubs into the playoffs. Oh what a day for Cub fans! By the way, Matt is a devoted follower of Jesus and a UPI guy.

Unsung heroes tend to be just that. They show up every day, work hard, and receive little recognition.

Some of the unsung heroes in the game are the wives.

Lisa Weston offers helpful insight into what it means to be a ballplayer's wife.

Mickey and I started out together in A ball, and we really did look at our baseball life as an adventure. Right then I don't know if I would have exactly chosen the path that God had for us, but it really was an adventure and we tried to look at it that way. I think the biggest thing, as well as the hardest thing, God taught me as a player's wife was to learn to be content, and I spent a lot of years struggling with that, just being content wherever we were.

There was a lot of pressure from college and my friends who were on their career paths for me to be somewhat independent. I really felt called to be with Mickey, and I was happy to do that, and support him, but there was a lot of pressure to be somewhere else and to do something else. I think my struggle with contentment was more wanting to be in the big leagues, and that was just not what God had planned for us. And so, it took the Lord really shaping me and molding me, and my trusting Philippians 4:6-8. You know what Paul said. "You learn to be content in any and every circumstance," and it was a great lesson for me as a baseball wife—to be content where we were.

I think the turning point for me personally, and Mickey would probably say the same, was the summer we spent in Syracuse. We had been up and down in the big leagues quite a number of times already, and we never seemed to stick. I just kept claiming Psalm 37:4-5, "Delight yourself in the LORD, and He will give you the desires of your heart. Commit your way to the LORD, trust in Him and He will do it." I thought delighting in the Lord for me would be that God would answer my prayer, and we would just settle in the big leagues kind of life. But that was not what God's will was, and so I needed to learn that when I delighted myself in the Lord, really desiring what He wanted, then I would be content with where He put us.

That summer in Syracuse Mickey was called up, and I went up to Toronto. We moved into a place to live; I drove back in the car that the Blue Jays gave the players. While Mickey went on a long road trip, I packed up the rest of our stuff. While I was on the way back to Toronto to pick up Mickey at the airport, Toronto made a big trade. The talk was that someone had to go down because the Blue Jays had traded for a big-name pitcher. And the only one on the team that still had options, even though he was pitching very well, was Mickey. I pulled into the airport and Mickey was standing there in his suit. I could tell by the look on his face that, yep, we were the ones that were going back down. We had to turn in our car and his stuff at the stadium. On that drive back we really struggled with being content and seeking what God had for us.

We went through a hard struggle for a month or so, and then Mickey received a letter. He had no idea who the writer was, but she wrote, "You signed Romans 10:9-10 on your baseball and because of that, I got to share those verses with my cousin, and she trusted in Christ." And then, Susan, whom he had never met, said, "You know, Mickey, I wish you were in Toronto, but because you weren't, Elizabeth heard the gospel, and her life was changed forever." I think that just hit both of us, me personally in a really big way to say, "You know what? God knew that we needed to be in Syracuse for the gal who trusted Christ." And so I began to look at every move we made—we played five or six more years after that—knowing that no matter where it was, God had put a circle of people around me (mostly women), for me to influence, share Christ with, and to live before. That became our focus: ministry in baseball. It really freed me to be content in whatever circumstance I was. I think that was probably the biggest lesson I learned as a player's wife.

The following devotional by Keeley Bowie (used by permission) expresses well the proper response of Christians to God's game plan for them, whether in ministry or as a ballplayer's family.

Be Brave

Do not be terrified; do not be discouraged,
for the Lord your God will be with you wherever you go
(Joshua 1:9 NIV).

A long time ago, at the beginning of our baseball career, I found a shirt with Joshua 1:9 on it. We were with the Braves organization at the time, so I just thought that was cool. As time passed and I began to experience the constant moving that comes with baseball, the challenge and promise of Joshua 1:9 came to be very special and very personal.

During the previous 16 years I estimate that we have moved about every three months. There may have been one year that we stayed in the same town for the entire baseball season. Other than that, though, we have been moved up, down, and sideways. And then, of course, there are the six-week stints for spring training. And the months of winter ball in the Dominican Republic during the off-season.

Believe it or not, when I was pregnant with our daughter, we moved *eleven* times and had *nine* different obstetricians. We met the doctor who delivered our precious first baby only 24 hours before she was delivered.

Change has been constant.

So now with our time in baseball seemingly over, I am not sure how to handle being stationary. There are so many positives to a "normal." Only one house payment and *no* rent! My children making friends and *not* having to move. Having *everything* unpacked.

I know that God is with me and I trust Him as I learn.

Prayer: *Thank You, Lord, for all the experiences you have blessed me with. Please help me to be brave as we transition out of our nomadic lifestyle.*

Our daughters have also been unsung heroes in the ministry of UPI. The first year of full-time ministry involved many days on the road.

At that time Amy and Lindsay were in fourth grade and kindergarten. It was tough for me to leave them so often, and frequently I would weep silently on the plane as I left my girls behind for those long trips. Carin did a great job of making up for the girls missing their daddy. She would encourage me with the fact that God was taking care of our girls. Carin wrote in the December newsletter:

> The girls miss their dad, but they really *want* him to be away if it means he's where God wants him to be. It's during the most difficult times I can see their spiritual eyes being opened, and during the loneliest times we are most aware of God's constant care and presence. Immanuel, God with us.

Recently I asked my daughters to describe what it was like growing up with a father in the ministry and frequently on the road. Amy, our oldest, gave me a paper she wrote during her freshman year in college. Her professor asked the class to write about their relationship with their fathers. This is what she wrote:

> From the moment I was born, I have had a sort of special relationship with my father. Instead of crying like most newborns in the delivery area, I let out a short whimper

Amy, Carin, and Lindsay

and instantly fixed my eyes on my father. I just gazed at him until finally the nurse had to take me. I can just hear his sarcastic response now, "Yeah, and then she didn't talk to me for a year."

As a little girl he was this bigger-than-life, immortal being. I can recall playing the ever so common game of "my daddy is better than yours because he can…" and always feeling like I had won. There wasn't anything he couldn't do or be. He'd spend hours and hours playing various made-up games and tickling me under my arms till my sides hurt. Sometimes I wondered if my friends were coming over to see me or my dad. After all, nobody else had a dad at 6'5" with spiked hair!

The only possible downfall I can think of was that my father traveled a lot. Sometimes up to five weeks at a time. He was the founder/director of the ministry that was growing rapidly that still had a very small staff. I remember hearing my mother tell someone that he had been gone 299 days that particular year. It was hard for me to understand why all my friends' fathers can be home for dinner every night and mine couldn't. There were many tears and disappointments during those times. However, it made seeing him all the more special and rewarding.

I remember counting the weeks that turned to days that would finally become minutes until he would step off the plane and walk in the front door. I would always be standing there, open arms, waiting for those big daddy bear hugs, while he anticipated hearing about everything that happened while he was gone. Those "quality" times meant a lot more than "quantity." He made a special point of taking me out on a special one-on-one date while he was home. Whether it was to the park or sitting in Dairy Queen, that was my time alone with Daddy. To this day, I still think it's one of the best things that a father can do with his child.

On those "dates" he would always make a specific point of asking me whether or not I still wanted him to be in the ministry or if it was too hard on me. He treated me like a real person. By that time I would be reflecting on my Dilly Bar or my new gifts from various countries he had just visited and would casually give him permission to carry on.

Another special time with my father while he was home was our prayer and devotional time every night before bed. We would start out with some sort of reading. Then we would thank the Lord for specific things pertaining to the day, confess any sins that we may have committed, and then say our prayer requests. He got me into a habit that I still practice today. His philosophy is that parents should have devotions with their children until about age 13, and then hope that they will continue on their own. Of course, by that age, I wanted to do them on my own.

As I got older, into my pre-teen and junior high years, my father's traveling and the concept of his being gone became a little easier for me. I began to realize that it was a privilege to have a father with such an exciting career and that with privilege comes some sacrifice. Plus, I knew how much he loved me unconditionally—he's always had a great way of expressing that—and that he would do just about anything for me. He says I had him wrapped around my little finger.

As my dad and I got closer and closer and that bond between us grew stronger, there was one thing that was getting worse. I'd always been a very well behaved child, but of course, as with all children, there were times when discipline was necessary. In our household, I was accustomed to my father being gone and my mother having to handle all discipline matters. In a sense, she had to be the bad guy all the time, and he got to come home and play super hero. Everything seemed fine to me until he decided one day I needed to be disciplined—by him. It was very hard for me to handle. I felt betrayed, and the truth is, I became very bitter and angry with him. I felt like screaming out, "How could you?" Or better yet, "How dare you?"

The next few years became very rocky for my dad and me. I became distant; he became concerned. I became rebellious; he became more concerned, and the cycle went on and on until one day he cornered me and everything broke loose. It went from backtalk and hysterics to tears and finally a good two to three hour talk that ended at 3 a.m. Since that day, words can't express the feelings I have for my father and the respect I have for him. A lot of the churning, physical and spiritual, has taken place in my life in the past three to four years. I attribute much of my spiritual growth to the good example my dad set. I'm able to trust and have faith in my heavenly Father because I've been shown such wonderful earthly love. It's almost hard for me to imagine a heavenly Father that can top the love I felt from my dad. He's also been a spiritual example in that he practices what he speaks—which is crucial for a child to see in her father. He's never failed to fulfill a promise or make exceptions to any rules or justifications for any wrong actions. He's taught me to fix my eyes on my heavenly Father just as I did on him my first day of life.

As I shared before, my father and I have always had a special unique kind of relationship. We both have the same warm sense of humor. We're so much alike that we can almost read each other's minds. We can be in the same room, and a simple glance with no words spoken can send us into a stark laughter. I can tell a joke or make a comment that no one else understands except for my dad—as if we have our own means of communication.

Lately I've been really getting to know my dad as a person. He still travels, but not as extensively as he used to. I'm the one that's hard to catch. However, as often as we both can, we still go out on our special dates just to catch up. I think it hurt him a little at first, but he knew when to step aside and let my boyfriend fill the role of my hero. It's such a blessing having a father who has the wisdom of a mature and distinguished gentleman and yet doesn't act or speak as if he was born in the dark ages. We talk as grown-ups now, sharing advice and opinions and discussing shared and opposing views on various issues.

What makes him so neat and makes me proud to say that he's my dad? He's an entrepreneur with a God-willing spirit. He's diverse and outgoing. He's talented and athletic. He's intelligent and witty. He's funny and energetic. He's firm and understanding. He's serious and sarcastic. He's sensitive and loving. He's God-fearing and humble. He's my dad—no, actually he's my daddy.

Here is what Lindsay wrote:

> My dad asked me to describe what it was like to have a father in the ministry and often away. I knew from a very early age the importance of ministry. I grew up with a "little me, big world" perspective that I am so thankful for. I knew that the most important thing my dad could do with his time was to tell others about Christ. I also knew what it meant to have a personal relationship with Christ. I understood how that relationship affected everything else in life.
>
> It was hard when my dad was gone on long overseas trips. I looked forward to his return with great anticipation. I had a very special relationship with my dad (and still do). He always made sure that my sister and I knew we were important and loved. I think because he traveled so much it made our time together even more special. He would have devotions and pray with me every night he was home. He would bring back special souvenirs from his trips that I treasured and joyfully showed off to all my friends. He would take me on "dates," and I cherished the time we spent together. I feel extremely blessed to have a dad that modeled God's unconditional love and made me feel so beautiful and special.
>
> When I was in high school, I had the privilege of going on a missions trip each year with UPI. It was something that

I have grown to appreciate more and more as I get older. I was able to travel and do things that most kids my age would never have been able to do. I had the opportunity to live with the people that we were ministering to, to meet missionaries and their families all over the world, to share my faith at a young age, and to see poverty and a way of life I had never seen before in our small town of Warsaw, Indiana. I loved watching the way people responded to my dad and the team with us as they learned about God's love. I was able to witness to others and see so many people come into a relationship with God through UPI.

I can't imagine growing up any other way. Our family didn't have a lot of money, but I never knew it. My dad was gone more than most of my friends' dads, but it never affected how close I felt to him. My faith in God and in His provision and plan for my life is so great now. I have an intimate relationship with my God and have experienced the joy of knowing Him my entire life. My perspective on life has been greatly influenced by the decision my parents made to follow Christ and by watching my dad's ministry as I grew up…and I am eternally grateful.

The testimonies of my daughters reveal something of the sacrifice of a family involved in ministry, and the players' wives give a glimpse of the struggles for the families of pro athletes. The lifestyle of a pro baseball player can be exciting. And ministry trips can be exhilarating, but behind the scenes there is sacrifice. There is much time away from loved ones and many missed milestones in their lives, like birthdays, ballgames, and family gatherings.

There are many unsung heroes in the baseball world as well as in ministry. There is sacrifice, but there is also joy when we know we are where God wants us to be. Often I've used the quote, "You can spend your life anywhere, but where will you invest it?"

It's Great to be alive because God is in control!

Action Points

- Are you simply spending your life somewhere, or are you investing it in something you believe in?

- What is your relationship with your family compared to your job? How would your family describe it?

Chopsticks and Fungoes

In my years of coaching, the fungo bat had become a treasured item. Designed for practice purposes, the fungo bat is used to hit directed fly balls and grounders in pregame practice. It is valuable tool for the baseball coach. Too thin for game use, it is perfect for making a coach look like he can actually hit fly balls. Whether in domestic or overseas camps, the fungo bat is a helpful tool. We had our fungoes and were ready to travel.

When baseball was added to the summer Olympic Games, opportunities opened up for UPI that were closed to other ministries. Mainland China had been a closed country to visitors for many years, but in the 1980s the door began to crack open for cultural exchanges between China and the United States. Countries like China were interested in developing a baseball program to compete in the Olympic games. They were receptive to UPI since we were willing to travel at our own expense and bring pro athletes who would teach baseball for free.

In May of 1985, UPI made its first trip to China. The team consisted of Bob Purdy, who was serving as a missionary in Hong Kong at the time; Dave Edler, first baseman for the Seattle Mariners; and me.

One of our first challenges in China was to attempt to use chopsticks, the eating utensils of the Chinese. We were told that to master the items, we should practice picking up shelled peanuts. At nearly every meal, there were peanuts, but only Bob Purdy really became proficient. That may be the result of years as a missionary in Hong Kong.

When we visited China, the country had eight teams, representing provinces that would be in consideration for international

Dave Edler and Tom Roy with driver, red flag limo, and translator in Beijing

competition. The teams spent nearly every day all year at the ballpark practicing, although they played very few games. We had the privilege of working with six of those teams in the cities of Beijing, Xian, Shanghai, Lanchou, Tianjin, and Chengdu. The people of China were very warm toward us, and we felt all the players and coaches truly appreciated our instruction.

From the time we arrived in Beijing until our departure two weeks later, we were treated with great respect. When our group arrived in Beijing, we were met by Mr. Hong, our host from the China Sports Service. (For their protection, names of our Chinese contacts have been changed in this chapter.) We were ushered into a "Red Flag" limousine, the most prestigious vehicle in China, reserved for dignitaries. We spent the whole day touring the area and feeling much more important than we were. That night we were treated to a special meal and then to the Beijing opera, a great honor. However, since the opera was in Chinese and since we were still in jet lag, we had trouble staying awake. When our friendly guide saw me sleeping, he smiled and said, "Oh, Tom is concentrating."

We left the opera early and went to the hotel, which was good by old Chinese standards. Our rooms were comfortable and complete with cockroaches. But we were quickly asleep. We awoke at five the next morning and took a walk through the streets of Beijing. Our senses were awakened to new sights, smells, and sounds. We watched shadow boxing in the park and walked through the early morning markets. Snakes, eels, pressed duck, and dogs in cages were all for sale and destined for someone's dinner table. Bicycles were everywhere, loaded with people and packages, hurrying through the streets and alleys. Instead of the sound of automobile horns there was a chorus of bicycle bells. We were keenly aware that we had entered a culture totally different from our own.

Later that morning we were driven in the red flag limo to the train station. We were ushered through a special gate and escorted to the first class section of the train. It was obvious they were keeping us isolated from the Chinese people.

Tianjin

When we arrived in Tianjin, the site of our first clinic, we were greeted as representatives of the United States. We were overwhelmed with the special treatment given us by the government of China.

Bob Purdy said our host, Mr. Hong, was one of the most open and talkative guides he had ever seen in China. He shared his opinions about China's policies, saying they changed so often it felt like a ping-pong game. Something that was allowed one day might suddenly be banned the next. He said there had been much spiritual and ideological pollution in Beijing in recent years. Foreign visitors would leave forbidden things behind like music and literature, including pornography. Young people who were caught listening to the music or dancing were put in jail for a minimum of five years. At the time of our visit some of the policies had just changed, including dance. Once illegal, it was now being taught in schools.

Our translator for the day was Mr. Chang who took us on a great tour of the area. Bob observed several changes: "Since my last trip into China in November, I can't believe how much the sunglass craze

Dave Edler, Tom Roy, and Bob Purdy in Tiananmen Square

has taken over. Almost everyone is wearing sunglasses, from the bus drivers to the farmers driving tractors." He noticed that blue jeans had become very popular as well.

We visited the Ming Tombs, with the 13 tombs of the 13 emperors and empresses. Most emperors were killed because of palace struggles. At the beginning of the Ming dynasty, around A.D. 1360, the capital of China was Xian, but later it was moved to Beijing. We saw the open tomb of Won Lee, the last emperor of the Ming dynasty, who had become emperor at age ten.

Next we visited the Great Wall, built 3,000 years ago and restored during the Ming dynasty. Parts of the wall are crumbling, and from the base it did not look too intimidating, but as we climbed we could see the incredible workmanship in this structure. The wall is approximately 3,750 miles long and 35 feet high at its highest point. At one time it was more than 6,000 miles long and wide enough for six horses. Mr. Chang also took us to see Tiananmen Square, the location of the tomb of Chairman Mao and the spot where demonstrators were massacred in 1989.

That evening, Mr. Jhou of the China Sports Service took us to The Original Peking Duck Restaurant. The king of Burma had been there the day before, and the food was excellent. During the meal we were told that China wanted to expand baseball and have UPI return.

Mr. Chang then took us to the Forbidden City, explaining that the lions at the gateway to the city were male and female—the male on the left and the female on the right. Both had raised paws with a ball under the male's paw, and under the female's paw was a lion cub on its back. Chang said this symbolized that the man controls the world, and the woman controls the family and the home.

He told us the following about China:

- If a worker's health is poor, he stays home and receives 60 percent of his wages.

- Popular sports in Beijing are soccer, ice-skating, and gymnastics, as well as watching basketball and volleyball.

- Each province and city has its own sports teams.

- Many schools teach martial arts and gymnastics to students ages 6-9.

- The government encourages one baby per family. Families with more than one are penalized, and in addition, they do not receive bonuses.

- If you have twins, you are not penalized, but you do not receive bonuses.

- If you only have one child, you receive a bonus until the child is 14.

- Mothers receive six months maternity leave with full wages. If the leave is extended to one year, she receives 75 percent of her wages.

- Bicycling is the main form of transportation. There are four million in Beijing alone and nine million in the surrounding area—one bike for every two people.

- Marriage requires a certificate from a government office along with a photo. A government official stamps the certificate and you are married.

- A ceremony with the girl's mother and the boy's father can be held later at any location.
- In the past marriages were always arranged.
- People in Beijing live in shared apartments that cost five yuan per month (less than $2).
- Sometimes apartments are shared by two newly married couples.
- Mr. Chang's living space was about 46 x 46 feet, which he shared with four other families. It had a common bathroom in the center.
- In China it is rare to find anything printed in English.
- A driver's license in China is called Four Papers. For each major accident or a traffic violation, one paper is taken away. If all four are lost within three years, the driver's license is taken away.

We asked Mr. Chang about religious freedom in China. He told us they were free to worship wherever they wished. We knew that was not true, but people were free to attend the Chinese run "Self Church."

A typical day for us in China began with a meeting with the sports VIPs in each area, followed by two hours of baseball instruction in the morning, lunch, and then two hours of instruction in the afternoon. We always worked through a translator. At the end of the day, we set aside time for the players and coaches to ask questions about baseball and life in the USA. We hoped to deepen relationships.

In Tianjin we met with a team that consisted of 25 players, ages 16-19. There was a middle school and an elementary school team as well, but they had a very limited playing schedule. We were told that the team plays about 30 regular season games and then tournaments begin, ending with a national championship game in May. The teams train nearly every day, including Sundays and most holidays. They attend classes in the morning, and they train in the afternoon.

Here are some stats about baseball in China:

- The average field size is 298' down the lines and 361' to the center field fence.
- They use aluminum bats because they cannot get enough good quality wood.
- They use mostly Japanese equipment, although some is made in China.
- The strike zone is from the base of the elbow to just below the kneecap.
- Pitchers throw fastballs, curve balls, and knuckle balls, but no change-ups and few sliders.

The coaches did not respond at first to our teaching, but as Bob Purdy stated, "It was obvious to see the pattern that took place—they began to realize that Tom and Dave did have something to offer. The players seemed to open up and become more excited, especially the pitchers."

At the end of the clinic we went back to the hotel, showered, and attended a special banquet given by the vice chairman for baseball of Tianjin, the deputy manager of Sports Services, and another man. Bob wrote, "It was very obvious that they were impressed, that they were pleased to have us there, not only for the promotion of baseball, but they were pleased with the way the clinics went and were very anxious that we should return."

They were especially interested in the possibility of our sending someone for three months or more to coach. They said if we could provide airfare to China, they would take care of all the expenses within the country, even for a family. The next morning, both leaders met us at the hotel and took us right to the train station. They gave us a very warm farewell.

Beijing

We arrived in Beijing, the capital city, and were told their baseball team was the best in China. They had two pitching machines plus some batting cages and screens—the best equipment we had seen.

Dave Edler teaches baseball to Chinese team.

They had a decent stadium, but the field was very rough. It was all dirt with a few patches of grass in the outfield. It was also bigger than most stadiums—approximately 328 feet down the line and 393 feet to the center. The stadium was a long way from the inner city, which made it almost impossible for fans to get there on bicycle to watch games.

The clinic with the Beijing team lasted from 1 to 5:30 p.m. with Dave starting off with a hitting exhibition. Bob reported, "The players were standing around the batter's box making 'oooh' and 'aaah' sounds. That gave him a lot of credibility and a captive audience." The only problem was that Mr. Chang was our only translator, so he had to run back and forth between my pitching instruction and Dave's hitting instruction. Consequently, there were long pauses in the instruction and a very winded translator.

Lanzhou

The most out-of-the-ordinary location for our clinics was Lanzhou. Bob's first impression of the Lanzhou area was, "It is all sand and clay and looks like a desert, but not quite like a desert. The people here had actually dug caves out of the hillsides to live in, incredible and fascinating. It reminds me very much of what the Middle East must be like, very much desert-like, yet hilly and with little green patches of rice fields here and there."

The former coach of this team was Mr. Blue. He was born in Shanghai and grew up playing baseball with children of American diplomats. His father was an English teacher, and Mr. Blue was very pro American. He believed the quality of American baseball and the teaching techniques were superior to the Japanese.

Mr. Blue invited us to his home, but later he apologized and said that although he very much wanted us to come, he was told he did not have permission. He had lost face. Later we learned that his father had been a Christian pastor in China before the revolution. We were very excited to hear that. Mr. Blue did not have the typical Chinese outlook on life.

The current coach was Mr. Tou, a former pitcher. He wondered why our stay was so short and would have liked us to stay longer, but we were on a six-city tour.

Lanzhou, we learned, had won the national championship in 1981 when Mr. Blue was the coach. After that he was demoted, which was typical in China, according to Bob. That practice is to keep any one person from coming into too much power. The Lanzhou team was now fifth in the nation, and player morale was low. Mr. Blue was frustrated with the players' lack of commitment, lack of discipline, and bad attitudes.

The team had 19 players and most of them modeled their hitting and playing style after Japanese baseball. The field was small, only 230' to right field and 328' to center. The field doubled as a soccer field, but it had a decent mound. The right field had an imposing wall, maybe a Chinese "Green Monster" like in Boston Red Sox Fenway Park. The *Gansu News* sent a reporter the day we were there, which was a first.

Our female translator, Ms. Pao, was a senior at the University of Lanzhou. She was a pleasant person but did not have any knowledge of the game or terminology of baseball. Because of the difficulty with translation, the clinic did not go as quickly or smoothly as we had hoped.

After the clinic the coach and players asked questions about American baseball. They wanted to know how it compared to Japanese baseball. They were all sitting around in a big circle with the three of us sitting in the middle. They wanted to know the length of the major league baseball season, when it began and ended, the number of games played each season, and the players' salaries. We told them Mike Schmidt was making two million dollars a year, which they could not believe. We answered questions about everything from Little League to the major leagues.

We learned that in 1982 an Australian baseball team made a trip to China and later a University of California team, which we thought might have been an Athletes in Action team. Also two rookie league coaches from the Dodgers organization had visited a few months before us. One of them was Ken Johnson.

Mr. Mai, the new coach, gave us a brief overview of baseball after the "liberation," which is what he called the revolution in 1949. He said baseball continued in China until 1961 when the Soviets started demanding a lot of money. Because of the economy, baseball was eliminated until 1974 when it was reinstated.

That evening we had the opportunity to work with his team on strategy. We taught first and third situations, stealing second, offensive perspectives, and defense. They were fascinated with our cut-off systems.

When we left, we were each given personal gifts like small teddy bears or pandas. I was given a gold and silver nail clipper. We appreciated these gifts because they were not government trinkets but were personal gifts.

Prior to leaving we were asked to give a short talk regarding attitudes. We spoke about what motivated us in baseball and in life. My talk was paraphrased Bible verses on attitude, teamwork, discipline, and motivation. Dave did the same, challenging them to understand what they wanted to achieve, to set goals, and to understand why they wanted to play baseball. It was well received, and Bob concluded our time with them with a challenge to work hard in baseball and to consider the claims of Christ. Later he wrote, "At this point, I just brought in very briefly the thought that God had created them and given them their abilities. Tom added that he wanted his life and everything he did to honor God."

Before leaving Lanzhou, we were taken to the night market. It was about ten blocks long, and there were clothes, chickens, fruits, nuts, shoe repair, and lots of sunglasses. We didn't see many foreigners, and people would stare at us or come up and touch us. With Bob's blond hair and blue eyes, Dave's red hair and hairy body, and my height (6'5"), I guess we stuck out in the crowd!

We were all impressed with a custom we called "Chinese hacking." It was common for people to cough and spit on the street. We became pretty good at sidestepping the spit. No wonder the Chinese are so talented in dance and gymnastics.

The evening before we flew home we had a very good discussion about God with our translator. She said she knew there was one God but that she did not believe in God. She did not think He could help her. She believed only in herself. She said, "I believe in me." Bob pointed out that this reflected much of the attitude in China. They were told what to do, they had been promised so much, and yet often they ended up with nothing.

We had a unique experience in another city. Early in the trip we had prayed for opportunities to share our faith. As we were leaving a clinic it began to rain, and the windows in the car steamed up from the humidity. Our translator was sitting in the passenger seat. This man, who had shown no emotion around us, began to write with his finger on the inside of the windshield. At first we thought he was writing some Chinese characters, but then we saw the letters G-O-D. I asked, "Do you mean 'good?'" He replied, "No, God." I asked him what he knew about the word "God." He wrote underneath, "God be with us." What a strange way to communicate, writing on a windshield! We wondered what it meant.

So we asked, "What does that mean to you?" He said, "Jesus." "How do you know about Jesus?" we asked. He said, "I know Jesus." We were amazed. We took a chance and told him we were Christians, too. He saw that Bob and I were wearing baseball hats with a cross logo. When he saw the logo on our hats he said, "Gorgeous, terrific, that's wonderful!" I gave him my hat. We asked him more questions, and he said an American student had given him "a little Bible," a New Testament. He said the student from America had asked him to pray to receive Jesus, and he did. We were amazed.

As we continued to talk with him we found out that his father was a very influential man in town, a member of the Chinese Communist Party. He also said he was not a good student in school and barely graduated. He called himself a "naughty boy." We were very aware of the risk he was taking to speak about his faith. We hope we were an encouragement to him.

Chengdu

Our forty-minute flight to Chengdu was interesting. The plane was vintage, with thin cracked vinyl seats that folded down. During our ascent the cabin filled with what looked like smoke. Next to me was a wealthy American woman who was terrified and thought we were going to crash, so I tried to comfort her. As it turned out, the "smoke" was just the cloud cover we were passing through.

We stayed at the Jinjiang Hotel and had beautiful rooms with new carpet and luxury we had not seen elsewhere in China. Few hotels in Chengdu were this nice. Chengdu was a city of four million people. Our first impression was that this city had much more color than the previous places we had visited. For the first time the clothing was colorful, and the children were dressed very nicely. It was an entirely different atmosphere and reminded Bob Purdy of Hong Kong.

We were told that the average factory worker made about 100 yuan per month, about $40. They have American movies with Chinese subtitles that cost about seven cents to attend. Our guide pointed out that food prices had gone up recently and had caused hardship for the people. We met a couple of men who wanted to exchange money with us. We were told that the black market and capitalism had hit Chengdu. Chengdu was China's model city for economics and had great influence. New products were available, and Western money was in demand.

Prior to conducting the clinics, we gathered with the coaches and officials and had tea, talking over the needs of the team. They told us the team had learned we were coming only two days prior to our arrival. We were surprised, as we had known we were coming months before. But this team had something very special, a video recorder, and they were able to record each of our clinics. There were 22 players on the team, six of whom were pitchers. Shanghai had taken first in the preliminary round with a 12 and 2 record, and Chengdu was second with a record of 11 and 3.

It was blazing hot, and we had a full morning of instruction. At noon we were served tea and a special eighteen-course meal of Szechuan food. There were bamboo shoots brought fresh from the mountains that day, heart of pig, eel, dumplings, and many other dishes we didn't recognize. It was excellent. Then they said we must rest and gave us each our own room with clean sheets. It was a welcome break.

Dave really had a great time with the hitters and gave baseball cards to each of them. He also gave away both his catcher's mitt and first baseman's glove that day. Those players were sharp, and Dave felt led by God to give them those meaningful gifts.

We had an interesting conversation in the van on the way to practice that morning. Dave asked our translator about the Buddhist religion, and in the conversation we were able to say that we were Christians. This man knew there was a church near his office and said he had once been inside the church. He knew some Bible stories. He said he had read some of the Old Testament and was familiar with some New Testament stories. He specifically mentioned the story about the salt losing its savor and the shepherd going to find the one lost lamb. However, he said he did not believe in anything.

The next day we were served another great meal—a modest four-teen-course luncheon. The time on the baseball field was rigorous, and we gave it our all. It was a good visit to Chengdu.

The final leg of the trip was to Shanghai. We arrived around 4 p.m. and were greeted by a man and a woman. The man was the head of the baseball federation, and the woman was the translator. Shanghai was similar to Hong Kong. The streets were narrow and crowded with bicycles everywhere. The population of the city was about 12 million. Our first impressions were feelings of warmth, friendliness, and energy. The city seemed to have a sparkle and skip in its step.

Beijing had its cultural relics, palaces, the Great Wall, and temples to the heavens. Tienjin was more of an industrial city. Lanzhou was a blue-collar place where the people worked very hard. Xian was a mixture. There was some old flavor, yet you could feel a sense of movement and change. While Beijing seemed to be the heart of the government, Shanghai seemed to be more the heart of the people with its culture and the arts. We were allowed time in each city to experience some of its history and culture.

We stayed at the Peace Hotel, which was very comfortable. We were thankful for this restful place, as it had been a long trip. Our first clinic was canceled because of heavy rains. Honestly, we were a little relieved to have some downtime. We were taken on tours of arts and crafts and cloisonné factories. After lunch we toured the Peaceful Hat factory. We entered the factory and took an industrial-size elevator to the seventh floor. When the elevator doors opened we found ourselves in the middle of a staff meeting. We were then taken to a side room and shown the various hats. I purchased 48 hats for UPI. They were made of corduroy, and I bought them for $1.60 each. What a deal! They delivered them to my room at the hotel the next day with the UPI logo and all.

We then visited a Children's Palace. These palaces provide after-school activities for the most gifted kids. It was in an old building that had been upgraded and divided into a number of rooms. A very polite little girl greeted us at the door. She took our hands and led us from room to room. An adult also accompanied us. In the first room a large choir entertained us. Next we went to a room of violin players and then watched a talented, young piano player. The tour continued from room to room with Chinese traditional instruments, drama, ballet, builders of model ships and planes, biology, electronics, computers, and math. It was pretty impressive.

The next morning, when it was time to get back to the ball field for the clinic, Dave was feeling really sick. Something Dave had eaten was not agreeing with his stomach. He would not be going with us that day, which meant we had to adjust our plans on the field. I had to demonstrate and teach both pitching and hitting. It is no surprise that I was not as impressive as Dave. Bob Purdy wrote, "Tom actually made contact with the ball, hitting line drives, but of course he didn't have the power Dave has." The field was wet that day and we were tearing it up, so we cut the session short. Our interpreter was not happy that he had to walk on the field and get his shoes and pant legs wet. Because of the rain, we were not able to do another clinic.

Dave was still feeling sick when he got home to the U.S. and later learned he had picked up an intestinal parasite that can survive in frozen temperatures...from eating ice cream in Shanghai.

At the end of the trip Bob reported,

It was interesting to see the pattern of the trip, starting with the short time we had in Tienjin, where we made such an incredibly positive impact in such a short time—where they gave us the banquet and were so glad that we were even there—to our profitable time in Beijing where we had a good contact. They were cordial; they were glad to learn about pitching, but there just wasn't much enthusiasm there. They were really interested in competition and not much in instruction and fundamentals. From there we went to Lanzhou where we received a warm welcome and had just a great time the whole time there. Tremendous response: coaches coming to our rooms and going over plays—just super contact with a very open door for the future. Then to Xian where we had a terrible time with their interpreter and with the sport service in general because of the presence of an Australian coach. But we were warmly received by the team itself when we had the afternoon clinic with them. They were quick to invite us back. Even in the short time, we still feel they were being more than just polite. Then on to Chengdu where again we had an extremely positive time. They took advantage of every possible moment, and the players seemed to take the most from the instruction. We finally ended in Shanghai, where we again wrapped up on a very, very positive note.

In each city we visited we were welcomed and treated with great honor. But we were seldom left without an "escort" and were always conscious of how the government controls every aspect of life in China. Although we had known we would not be permitted to speak openly about our faith, we were encouraged by the opportunities we were given to speak about what motivates us in life and by the few private conversations we had with individuals. It was apparent that although there is repression of religion in China, God is very much at work in that vast country.

As we left China, Bob picked up a copy of the *Peoples Daily* newspaper. An article in that paper mentioned that baseball would perhaps become an Olympic sport in 1988 and that China was very anxious to raise its standard of baseball. It was a thrill for the three of us to have this small role in helping China become a country of baseball. Who would have thought that in 2008 China would host the Olympics and field a baseball team? Mostly we were thankful for the opportunity to sow seeds for Jesus. What an honor to be ambassadors representing the United States, but even more, ambassadors for Christ. We wondered what other unique opportunities God had in our future.

It's Great to be alive because God is in control!

Action Points

- Please pause right now to thank God for the freedoms we enjoy.

- Please pray for China. Our God is not limited by governments or any other powers.

- How might God open up opportunities even in impossible situations in your life?

Expanded Strike Zone

Because of my increased travel Phil Menzie took on more responsibilities, including traveling solo to spring training and setting up some of the summer clinics. Milwaukee, Detroit, Philadelphia, New York, Dallas, Chicago, and Akron all had a keen interest in doing the outreaches. The clinics that summer went well. Here are a few quotes from some of the players that participated:

> I really received a blessing from helping Tom and Phil with the clinic in Philadelphia. I look forward to being able to serve the Lord through UPI in the future.
> *Lee Tunnell, Pittsburgh Pirates pitcher*

> I have done a lot of baseball clinics before, but never one that had me share my faith at the conclusion. Unlimited Potential clinic outreach is fantastic and a wonderful way to reach children and adults.
> *Bob Knepper, Houston Astros pitcher*

> Tremendous outreach to souls through baseball. It's been encouraging to have opportunity to share my faith through UPI and has meant a lot to me as a pro baseball player.
> *Chris Bando, Cleveland Indians catcher*

> I'm grateful that Unlimited Potential is reaching out to where kids are. This is a great way to reach people for Christ.
> *Craig Reynolds, Houston Astros shortstop*

In addition to China, other doors were opening in the Far East and in November of 1985 we took our first missions trip to Korea. Missionaries Bill and Bonnie Sutherland hosted us and Glenn and Theresa Davis made the trip. Theresa, who was born in Korea and moved to the states as a young girl, longed to return to her homeland. Glenn had just completed his first full seasons in the big leagues and was growing in his love of Jesus. Korea was the perfect place for his first missions trip.

Glenn asked UPI for help to put his story into a tract format. Kent Fishel did the writing and Carin designed the cover. Glenn called it "From Hell to Houston." It was the first time we had attempted anything like it, and Glenn was excited for the opportunities it gave him to be a witness for Christ. Here's the full tract.

"From Hell to Houston"
Glenn Davis

"Living in Hell" would best describe my early life. At seven, my parents separated and later divorced. From that time on, I began to experience the emotional hostilities that came from the conflict between my parents.

Survival became a way of life for me. Because of physical and mental tormenting by my parents, along with my own rebellious actions, I sought refuge wherever I could find it. Sometimes I slept in the park; at other times different neighbors would take me in for the night. I did not know what the meaning of love was. Often I got mixed up with the wrong crowd because I wanted to feel accepted by others.

As the pressures of life came down on me, I contemplated suicide. Several times I held a gun to my head or a knife to my stomach, but I just couldn't kill myself. Sports became my life. It was the only thing that I wanted to live for.

During my childhood days, I was wild. Fighting, destruction, and terrorizing people were all I cared about. As a delinquent kid, I was involved in robberies, vandalism, and constant trouble at school—earning the reputation of being the meanest guy in the neighborhood.

At age 17 I left home. George Davis, my high school coach, and his family opened their home to me and took me in as part of their family.

All of this time I lived two lives. It began at the age of 8, when I was told by my Sunday School teacher to go forward and ask the preacher to save me. One Sunday morning I followed my friends to the front of the church. After this, I didn't think about Christ until I was 16. While lying in the hospital with a broken arm, afraid that my baseball playing was finished, I again reached out to Jesus and asked Him to heal me. After this, I went my own way without Christ.

While living with the Davis family, I noticed that though they loved Jesus Christ and lived for Him, they never forced me to conform. I continued my hypocritical ways of talking about being a Christian, even though I didn't walk what I was talking.

In college, I changed my ways. I began to find other ways to occupy my time. I started partying, continued my drinking, and looked to girls for sexual satisfaction. After attending one year at a junior college, with money running out, I signed a contract with the Houston Astros.

At the age of twenty, I was living life in the fast lane. After signing a good contract, I had a lot of money in my pocket. I bought a new sports car, lived on a golf course in a luxurious condominium, and bought a lot of nice clothes. It seemed like everyone wanted to be my friend, but all they wanted was a part of my lifestyle. I thought I was having a lot of fun, but with the fun came a lot of responsibility. Playing in the minor leagues was a new experience. Everyone was fighting for a position; there was always pressure to produce.

It was easy to join teammates at the bars—drinking, carousing, and chasing women became the thing to do.

Eventually I got tired of this wild lifestyle. The stress of baseball and the desire to keep up with the crowd got so bad that I couldn't sleep at night. I searched for peace of mind, love, and joy. I had no assurance of tomorrow, and there was no security in life for me. No matter what I tried I couldn't find happiness. Life had no meaning for me. My search for happiness was like a vapor. It was there for a little while, then vanished. I needed something solid to replace the emptiness within.

After my second professional season, my chapel leader confronted me with the fact that my so-called Christian character wasn't fooling anyone—least of all, God. Yes, I was a hypocrite living in sin—on my way to Hell. As God's spirit came on me, I felt tremendous fear. I knew that if I were to die that night I would be held accountable by God for my life. Not knowing which way to turn, and facing continued torment in my life, I had to make a decision.

At that point, I felt the presence of God and began to cry. It seemed like every sin I ever committed was going through my mind. There on the steps of my home, I cried out to God and asked Him to save my life.

I prayed, admitted my need to be forgiven, confessed my sins, and asked Jesus Christ, the Son of God, to take complete control of my life. What a change I experienced in my life! It was like a ton of bricks had been lifted from my shoulders. I had finally found the love and peace of mind I had been looking for. Jesus made my life worth living again.

No, life hasn't always been easy as a Christian. Pressures still come. But as I yield to Him in every situation, I have learned that I can always count on Him to see me through.

You, too, can experience the joy of knowing Christ as your personal Savior and trust His power to see you through the daily struggles of your life.

Please carefully consider the following four points from God's Word.

1. God loves you and has a wonderful gift for you.
   John 3:16: "For God so loved the world that He gave His one and only Son, that whoever believes in Him shall not perish but have eternal life."
   Rom. 6:23: "For the wages of sin is death, but the gift of God is eternal life in Christ Jesus our Lord."

2. You can't get to His gift of eternal life on your own.
   Eph. 2:8, 9: "For it is by grace you have been saved through faith – and this not from yourselves, it is the gift of God – not by works, so that no one can boast."

3. You need to come into a right relationship with God in order to receive this gift of eternal life.
   John 5:24: "I tell you the truth, whoever hears My word and believes Him who sent Me has eternal life and will not be condemned."

4. God sent Jesus Christ to be your way to experience forgiveness of sins and eternal life.
   2 Cor. 5:21: "God made Him who had no sin to be sin for us, so that in Him we might become the righteousness of God."
   1 Tim. 2:5: "For there is one God and one mediator between God and men, the man Christ Jesus, who gave himself as a ransom for all men."
   Pray and ask Jesus Christ to forgive you of your sins, yield every area of your life to Him, and receive Him as your Savior and Lord.

Glenn was well known in baseball and we were warmly received as we arrived at the Korean ballparks. One event from that trip stands out in my mind. Glenn and I were asked to put on a clinic for a Korean professional team, the Bears. We were very excited for this opportunity because the professional teams were revered by the fans and difficult to reach. It was a privilege to be invited to their ballparks.

After accepting the invitation, Glenn and I realized we needed uniforms. We had been conducting clinics in shorts and T-shirts, but

Astros' first baseman Glenn Davis speaks though translator in Korea.

this was a pro team. In the 80s the Astros uniform had multicolored stripes. We found a Korean tailor, were measured, and Glenn tried his best to describe the Astros uniform. It wasn't exact, but 24 hours later we both had uniforms. As we took the field at the stadium, Glenn was asked to teach hitting and I was to work with pitchers.

Glenn stepped into the batter's box and the Korean players positioned themselves around the batting cage. As we began the session, it was obvious Glenn was struggling with his first couple of swings. After days of travel and teaching clinics, there had been few opportunities for him to swing a bat. Now in front of a professional audience he wanted to put on a good demonstration. We both prayed silently as he took a few more practice swings.

Suddenly I felt that I should draw the attention of the players away from the hitting to focus on the fundamentals. I asked the players to watch Glenn's feet, then to move up to his knees, waist, shoulders, hands, and his head. By that time Glenn had taken another 15 to 20 swings and was ready to hit. He asked the pitcher to throw the ball at batting practice speed. The pitcher was naturally excited to pitch to a current major league baseball player so the baseballs came in a little faster than batting practice, but that was no problem for Glenn. He hit the first ball out of the park beyond left field, and then continued to hit 10 to 15 home runs, each farther than the previous one. The players were impressed and some even bowed to him. God had provided the power and ability needed for just that moment.

Next it was my turn. This old man was nowhere near the athlete that Glenn was, but I was prayerfully confident that I could teach pitching. However, based on Glenn's performance they wanted me to take the mound and pitch. To say I prayed would be an understatement. I nervously took to the pitching rubber and began a few practice throws. What could I show these professional pitchers?

It came to my mind that I would teach them change-ups. For sure I could throw the ball slow. For those readers who are not familiar with pitching, a change-up is a pitch that comes out of the hand like a fastball, but has less velocity and more movement. The intent is to deceive the batter, thus throwing him off stride. In watching a few games in Korea I had noticed that the pitchers had decent arm strength, some had good curve balls, but I never saw a change-up. So the lesson began and I prayed that God would give me the ability to communicate how to throw each pitch, but also the ability to throw strikes.

I demonstrated five different grips for change-ups and threw low strikes with almost each one. The circle change was moving down and away from the hitters. The palm ball was doing just what it was supposed to do and the split finger split. The pitching coach was very happy and now each pitcher attempted to throw the various change-ups. To say the least, the entire day was a success on the baseball field. Once again God answered prayer in a big way.

After the clinic we were invited into the "holy of holies" of the Korean baseball world, the locker room. We drank soup and ate other unfamiliar foods as we talked with the players about life and our faith in Jesus. It was a great first opportunity to share baseball and Jesus at that level. Years later we learned that one of their players made a commitment to Christ shortly after our visit. You never know where God will work.

Glenn Davis, right, with UPI guys Atlee Hammaker and Dave Dravecky

Wikipedia says this about Glenn:

Glenn (born March 28, 1961 in Jacksonville, Florida) is a former first baseman in Major League Baseball, who played with the Houston Astros (1984-90) and Baltimore Orioles (1991-93). He batted and threw right-handed. Davis played one season at the University of Georgia before signing a minor-league contract with the Houston Astros.

He began his major-league career with the Astros in 1984, in which he finished 5th in the National League rookie of the year voting. He was an all-star in 1986, winning the Silver Slugger award and finishing 2nd in the MVP voting as the Astros narrowly missed reaching the World Series. He would finish in the top 10 in MVP voting in both 1988 and 1989, establishing himself as one of the best power hitters in the league.

In 1992, Davis founded The Carpenter's Way, a home for troubled children in Columbus, Georgia. He currently serves as an elected city councilor for the city of Columbus.

Chris Bando, right, and Tom Roy dine with an American family in Bangkok.

The last trip of 1985 was to Bangkok in December. Chris Bando of the Cleveland Indians had committed to make the trip and once again British Air was providing the flights. Chris and I were to meet in Chicago, then on to New York, London, and Bangkok. But CB's flight into Chicago was delayed and we missed our connection to New York by eight minutes because God had other plans.

The British Air agent found us another flight to New York. We arrived at Newark at 1:00 a.m. and our flight to London left from JFK at 9:30 a.m. The only transportation available at that hour was a limo. The limo driver's name was Rick and during the 45-minute ride between airports we had a great conversation with this man. He was full of questions and by the time we arrived at the JFK airport, Rick had prayed to receive Christ! Although we had stayed up all night, we now knew why God had re-routed us in New York.

In order for us to be in London in time to make our Bangkok flight, British Air put us on The Concorde. The flight was 3 hours and 18 minutes to London, arriving in time to catch our flight to Bangkok and arriving there ahead of our original flight from New York. Never again would a UPI trip include that kind of speed and comfort: first class gray leather seats and a silver vase with a rose at every seat.

Highlights of the Trip

- Wendy, age 18, who had attended a clinic the year before, trusted in Christ. She attended church with us on Sunday and youth group Wednesday night. She is now actively involved in church.

- We were able to see some fruit from the previous year, represented in the lives of some of the coaches and players.

- We spent 56 hours on the baseball field with about 200 kids. Twenty-one made first time professions of faith in Christ.

- A special group of players, including 15 Thai kids who were new to the game of baseball, came to the clinics. At the invitation (translated into Thai) five of these Buddhist young men trusted in Christ alone for their salvation.

- The national coach for the country of Malaysia asked us to come to his country to teach baseball and share our faith.

- Several local Thai corporations covered all expenses for this trip, more than $17,000, which was a huge blessing.

The UPI ministry was thriving but the finances were barely sufficient. It was obvious that if this ministry was going to make it, God would have to provide. After much prayer I sensed God telling me that He was going to take care of that area so that no man could take the credit for it. I strongly sensed I was to stop asking and just do what God had called us to do. He was stretching me; calling me to truly live by faith.

It was apparent by now that we could not do the ministry alone. We needed both the prayers and the financial support of other believers around the globe. Specific prayer needs were listed in the UPI newsletter and a prayer chain was established for the staff and board. In his book, *The Principles of Prayer*, published by BMH Books, Pastor Ivan French relates what happens when we become prayer partners.

- Interests are enlarged.
- Sympathies are deepened for others.
- Spiritual sensitivity is sharpened.
- Genuine JOY is experienced.
- Christ-like character is enhanced.

Prayer is important communication with our Provider and Protector. It is important to keep an eye on the goal with an ear connected to the Giver of the ministry. We are so grateful to all who pray for this ministry. We will probably never know in this lifetime what a difference those prayers have made. "The prayer of a righteous man is powerful and effective" (James 5:16).

By 1985 we had a basic schedule in place for each year:

- January - Puerto Rico
- February - office time
- March - Spring Training
- April - visit teams in home cities
- May - August - camps and clinics
- September - December - international trips
- November - attend PAO Baseball Conference

It's Great to be alive because God is in control!

Action steps

- What part does prayer play in determining God's will in your life?

- Is prayer your last or first resort?

- Have you ever asked God to bring people to you for the purpose of sharing your faith with them?

10

Road Trips

With many opportunities ahead of us and little experience behind us, we moved forward, learning along the way.

In 1986 UPI moved out of the basement office into rented space. It had been previously occupied by a pediatrician, and the office walls were painted with Disney characters. The back room had Goofy on the wall so I knew that was not going to be my office (even though "Goofy" had been used to describe me upon occasion). People who came in would wonder what kind of Mickey Mouse ministry this was. It was a humble space but it still holds great memories.

One day a traveling evangelist, Dr. Smith, visited my little office. I had been sitting there wondering exactly what God wanted me to do. After months of heavy travel there were suddenly a few empty weeks on the calendar. I felt like I was wasting God's time and money just sitting there. Dr. Smith sat and listened. He told me that in ministry there will be times when no one calls, but eventually someone will call and when they do, I will need to be ready. He said God's timing is not man's timing and that ministry is not measured in time but in people. He reminded me that if one life is rescued, all our waiting is worth it. Many times since then I have needed that reminder. It wasn't long before the calendar filled up.

Soon it became necessary to hire a secretary to handle the office workload. Paul Refior resigned as chairman of the board and Terry Harnish became the chairman. Both men added much with their leadership skills and commitment to ministry. It was a time of growth and change, and it was good to know that God was in control.

During Spring Training in March of 1987 Carin and I were driving from Tucson to Phoenix. We stopped in Casa Grande where I had reported for spring training with the Giants about 20 years earlier. It was the first time I had visited Casa Grande since being released, and I was flooded with memories. I had been only eighteen and it was my first trip out of Wisconsin. I remembered flying into Phoenix where a bus took a group of us rookies to Casa Grande. I was in awe back then to be in the same facility as great players like Bobby Bonds, Juan Marichal, and Willie Mays.

I stood on a balcony looking out over the complex where the fields had been. Some of the buildings were still there, vacant and neglected, but most of the fields were gone. The hotel had been recently remodeled and a golf course had replaced some of the fields. Carin and I were struck by the fact that a career in professional baseball is temporary at best. Like those fields, even the best players fade and are forgotten. God had moved me on from baseball to something that would not fade.

After the spring training visits, I traveled to the Christian college tournament in Florida that Norm Wilhelmi organized each spring break. UPI was now involved in the tournament each year, bringing pro players to speak. That year the speakers were Glenn Davis, Jose Alvarez, Jeff Calhoun, Tim Burke, Carlos Rios, Marty Clary and Tim Cash, a young man I would come to care about very much. The college players listened intently as the pros shared their personal experiences in baseball and in their faith. Afterward, there was a question and answer time, which gave the college players an opportunity to interact with the pros. I am confident there is no tougher audience than college athletes, but these guys were locked in.

That summer proved to be another full one. A new clinic location was added to the lineup. John Weber, who served as chaplain to the Texas Rangers, had arranged our first clinic in Texas. Five hundred and fifty young people attended and nine pro athletes taught baseball and shared their testimonies. The U.S. division of UPI had hit full stride.

Jake Boss, with the help of Huntington College coach Mike Frame, orchestrated the first UPI baseball camp at Huntington College. There were 42 campers including 10 kids from Puerto Rico who flew in to attend the weeklong baseball camp. UPI now had baseball camps in British Columbia, Grace College, Huntington College and Camp of the Woods in upstate New York.

A few years earlier, a young man named Tim Dell had come to Christ at the Okanagan Major League Baseball Camp. Tim attended The Kings College outside of New York City on a baseball scholarship. After his first year Tim transferred to Huntington College, which is about 45 minutes from Warsaw. He pitched well at Huntington and was drafted by the Philadelphia Phillies in the 12th round. I was a part-time scout for the Phillies at that time and my boss, Tony Lucadello, really liked the upside of Tim's pitching. He played a few years with the Phillies farm clubs and then found himself with the Brewers. Tim has remained a good friend.

Ministry opportunities are often built on relationships. Such was the case with Bob Purdy. After spending time together in Hong Kong and China, Bob made it possible for Carin and me to spend a week at Camp of the Woods in upstate New York. Bob's father was the director and Bob had grown up at the camp. Bob knew the travel demands of UPI and thought we needed some time to relax together. It was a kind offer, but all I could imagine was a week living in a tent, cooking over a campfire and swatting mosquitoes.

Well, Camp of the Woods was nothing like what I had envisioned. It is a beautiful lakefront resort in the Adirondack Mountains that provides a true vacation. It offers recreation and relaxation as well as outstanding Bible teaching. We had a great week together, enjoying the scenery and the speakers. The following year we were asked to return to offer a baseball camp as part of the program. UPI continues to conduct a baseball camp for two weeks each summer at Camp of the Woods. This allows a staff member time away with family and a chance to sit under great teaching. What a great summer for UPI.

Carin wrote the following for the newsletter:

For Mother's Day this year Tom bought me a tree. He said it was to remind me of him—every fall it leaves.

Fall is here, the leaves are falling, and Tom is leaving again. He flew to Korea on October 10 with four pros: Harold

Reynolds and Dave Valle of the Seattle Mariners, Jose Alvarez, Atlanta, and Mickey Weston, New York Mets. After outreaches in Seoul and a brief stop in Hong Kong, Dave, Jose, and Mickey will return home and Harold will accompany Tom to Japan, Taiwan, and Manila. Other trips for Tom this fall will include Africa, Thailand, and The PAO conference. Because of this, we're really grateful for the chance we had to travel with Tom this past summer.

Many of you have asked how the girls and I get along while Tom is away. The answer is fine. Really! So many of you have told me you pray for us while he is away. That's the main reason we're fine. There are many times we are highly conscious of your prayers as we see God caring for us. We're so thankful you care enough to pray.

Also, Tom has decided to limit his trips to three weeks maximum unless family is with him. Between trips he takes the girls out on dates. Whenever possible we try to travel with him. We try to make the best use of the time we do have together. All these things help make the times apart easier.

Another question we often hear is, "What do you do while Tom is away?" Here are some of the jobs I believe God has given me.

Stability. With Tom's schedule, someone needs to be home to provide a sense of consistency and structure for the girls, and keep things running smoothly (sort of) at home.

Availability. It is my desire to be available for Bible studies, speaking, and any other areas God may choose to use me.

Encouragement. The girls and I try to become cheerleaders. We try to encourage him and each other.

Prayer. We pray daily for Tom's safety and strength, for effective outreaches for the men who travel with him—and for their families. (I'm especially sensitive to the needs of the pro families because they also know what it's like to say many good-byes during the year). We also pray for you.

In 1986 Jose Alvarez, former pitcher with the Atlanta Braves, made his first trip to Korea with UPI. Team members on that trip were Dave Valle, Harold Reynolds, Mickey Weston and me. We stayed at the Seoul Gardens Hotel, which was very nice but not a luxury hotel by any stretch. The beds were very small and my first response was to wonder how in the world we would fit. It could end up being a long night with little sleep.

This was Jose's signal to pull one over on me. Using the lobby phone he called my room and in his best Korean accent asked for "Massah Loy," which is how the Koreans at the front desk said my name. "This is Yung Soo," he said. "I have good news for you. You too tall so we put you in top floor penthouse suite. You will enjoy very much. Come to front desk and get key."

I bought it. I was pumped and told the team that we all were going to be upgraded to the top floor so they needed to start packing. Obviously, when I got to the front desk there was no Mr. Young Soo and no upgrades. I had been had. It was one of many times I was fooled by guys on trips.

Alvin Davis, Tom Roy, and Dave Valle; early days with the Seattle Mariners

Dave Valle, catcher for the Seattle Mariners, wrote: "This past week has flown by–telling everyone of the mighty works of God. I still can't believe it. It was great. Imagine God using me! What an honor! He sure is an equal opportunity employer in His service."

Jose says, "I remember great times of devotions on these trips. Tom had a servant's heart and could connect no matter the surroundings. He had a great ability to lead, organize and gather the troops. He is easy to follow naturally because of who he is. He does not force anything on you."

That's nice but it sounds self-serving. How about this: Baseball and practical jokes seem to go together, but guys like Glenn and Jose also have great ministry hearts. They relate equally well to kids and college players and work long hours with no complaints.

In December we took coaches to Puerto Rico and then to the Dominican Republic. It was a great time of ministry with instructors who knew the routine as we entered new territory. Good friend and outstanding college coach Sam Riggleman joined Jake Boss, Pastor Bob Stoner and his wife Robin, Bob Purdy, and me for the trip to Puerto Rico. Pro athletes that helped out included Jose Alvarez, Steve Hammond, and Carlos Rios. Jose and Carlos both became great friends of UPI and ambassadors for Christ within the game of baseball.

Pastor Bob Stoner of Millersburg, Pennsylvania, wrote the following about his UPI trip:

> UPI's baseball ministry mission to Latin America has played a dynamic role in developing the heart of this Pennsylvania pastor. I've been privileged to be sent by my congregation to share my love of the Lord with my love of baseball before young and old in the Caribbean countries.
>
> God's presence was felt as we united with Pablo Seibenmann and the team of Baptist missionaries, and we taught baseball and saw many respond to Jesus. The need there is great. Many children cannot identify where they live. Others point out small dwellings, crudely erected against a wall of a baseball park in a 10 by 10 space with no water or sewage.

We must pray for the ongoing work of these missionaries as they impart the gospel.

The second leg of our trip saw us say goodbye to Bob Purdy and welcome Harold Reynolds, the effervescent second baseman of the Seattle Mariners. Harold is no stranger to UPI trips, and his presence was a delightful spark, as we launched into Venezuela for our first baseball outreach there. The Evangelical Alliance Mission coordinated our efforts, and coordinate they did. As a pastor, I was privileged to share in churches and teach outfield skills while testifying of God's work in my life. These people put much prayer and preparation into our mission and God greatly rewarded them. Our prayer life was challenged when we returned to our room night at night. God poured out His Spirit on us, and we were humbled to be used by Him in a most special way.

As our ten-day experience came to an end, over 600 first time conversions were claimed, with both countries well prepared with follow-up teams. Churches were ready to invite these people into their fellowships. Discipleship teams were ready to go into homes to further witness. We of the UPI team were dynamically in awe of our Majestic God, and His desire to include us in His work. Because of this experience, I will never be the same as a pastor or as a coach. God has taken me by the hand and shown me how He wants to work. Play ball. Bring on the opposing team, because in Christ, we are all victorious.

The following year UPI bought its first computer. As the ministry expanded it was needed. Today it is difficult to imagine an office without a computer.

Jake Boss continued to expand the camps, launching the first baseball camp in the history of Nova Scotia, Canada. Overseeing the camps was hard work but Jake did a great job. Five thousand five hundred kids came through UPI camps and clinics during the summer of 1987.

That fall we returned to Korea. Seoul was gearing up for the Olympic summer games and the city was beautiful. Glenn Davis, Alvin Davis, Tim and Christine Burke, and Carin and I went on that trip. The Burkes had been friends since the minor leagues; they had been great supporters of the work of UPI and they both had a passion to share Christ.

Tim and Christine were in the process of adopting a baby from Korea through an adoption agency, and although their baby girl had been born in August, they knew it would be many months, possibly years, before the paperwork was completed and they could bring her home. Until then she was placed in foster care at an unknown location, but they were excited to visit the country of their daughter's birth.

The Burkes contacted the adoption agency when they arrived and learned that their baby had shown slight signs of jaundice, so she had been brought to the hospital in Seoul for observation. In God's perfect timing she arrived at the hospital the same day our plane landed in Seoul. Carin and I accompanied Tim and Christine to the hospital to meet Stephanie, their first child. Because of the personal contact with the adoption agency officials, the paperwork

Tim and Christine Burke visit an orphanage in Korea.

was rushed through and they were able to bring their new baby home by Christmas.

During that trip we were able to visit an orphanage that cared for "unadoptable" kids, all with handicaps, and a Baptist orphanage where the children were living in tents until funds could be raised to build proper housing. There were many orphans in Korea at the time, some the children of American servicemen. Korea is a country of beautiful people with strong cultural traditions. In Korea a child's identity is from the father, so those children without fathers had no place in Korean society. We wanted to bring them all home. It was difficult to say good-bye but great to know that what we had to offer them was far better than a home. We shared with them the hope for a home in eternity. There were also opportunities to speak in schools and to visit military bases.

On UPI trips we try to meet each morning for a time in the Word and in prayer. In one of those prayer times Alvin Davis was overwhelmed with the need he saw all around him and he wept as he prayed, asking God to open up opportunities to share the hope of Christ. We saw God answer that prayer in some amazing ways on

Tom Roy speaking in Korea; seated: Jose Alvarez, Glenn Davis, Tim Burke, Alvin Davis

that trip as many young people responded to the gospel. Missionaries Bill and Bonnie Sutherland also arranged for the wives to speak for some women's groups.

While we were in Korea, Carin experienced some of the same emotions I have had on trips, being so far from home. When you realize you are on the opposite side of the globe, you feel helpless if anything should happen to your family and you are needed. Bonnie Sutherland could identify with that feeling and was able to offer encouragement with a verse that had meant much to her. In Numbers 11:23 God asks Moses, "Is the arm of the Lord too short?" (NIV). I had to learn to trust my family to the arms of the Lord.

Opportunities continued to come in and UPI was being stretched. But by the end of 1987 UPI was $7,000 in the black. Since that time God has faithfully provided for all the expenses of UPI.

One of my favorite memories was the time I challenged Norm Wilhelmi to attend the World Sports Ministry Conference with me in Seoul, Korea, in 1988, just before the Olympics. More than five hundred delegates from a hundred nations were represented. This was a time for training sports ministries to work with world-class athletes like Olympians. It was the first time Norm had been to Asia since his days in the Navy in WWII. Norm was in his sixties and I wanted him to see how God was working through sports to advance the gospel around the world.

He says, "I didn't really want to go but got talked into it." Norm is a big man with a gruff exterior but he has a big heart. He remembers, "We rode to the hotel, cramped in a cab big enough for a midget." Norm tells the story of his world being enlarged and touched:

> One morning I sat across from a guy from Africa, Mahinja— can't think of his last name. He told me a story about how he'd walk many miles with his soccer team to play a game, so he could tell the opponents about Jesus. They had one badly worn ball—if one of his guys remembered to bring it—for the game. I met Mahinja several times that week and was really impressed at his dedication and his ministry, using nothing to tell the Jesus story. I got hooked.

One day I went down the street to the Itaewon market and bought eight soccer balls and brought 'em up to his hotel room. You'd have thought I just gave him and his buddies a bushel full o' gold. I almost had to fight my way out of his room for the "thanks" that took all kinds of forms from those guys. To say the least, I was impressed by guys who had nothing and seemed overjoyed with God's Spirit. The trip awakened me to the power of sports and how "games" can be used so effectively in bringing the gospel to people of different cultures and languages.

Norm also remembers going to church in Seoul to hear Rev. Cho. We went to the third of seven services they held each Sunday. The service was translated into seven different languages and the offering was taken up from thousands of people in just twelve minutes. Norm got a bit emotional as they began to sing "How Great Thou Art." The words were in Korean, but the tune was the same. What an awesome experience to worship with people of different countries and cultures.

My role at the conference was to lead a few workshops. At the time most sports ministries were based in the United States, but today there are groups ministering to athletes around the world. Organizations like International Sports Coalition were taking off. It was great to be able to be a part of the conference, to be challenged from the Word, and to mingle with other sports ministries to discuss ways to partner with them on outreaches.

I returned from the conference on a spiritual high. The world had been opened to UPI, and we were ready to move ahead with full strength. The international side of UPI was exploding.

One of the disappointments of 1988 was the canceling of a planned trip to Cuba. Cuba has a great history of baseball and I was eager to go. We were ready. In fact, some of the players were already at the airport waiting to board their flight when we got word from our government that our visas had been denied. The men returned to their homes, disappointed, but God had another plan. Six years later, in June of 1994, we would be allowed to make that trip.

In 1989 UPI began sponsoring the National Christian College Athletic Association "UPI Award." I have had the privilege of serving as the chaplain for the NCCAA national college championship baseball tournament. The NCCAA was started in 1968 by Norm Wilhelmi to enable Christian colleges and universities to compete in an atmosphere of fair play and clean competition. The UPI award is given each year to a player who excels in the classroom and on the field and who demonstrates a life sold out for Christ. The recipients of this award are fine examples of young men who are refined in the fire of competition and who demonstrate Christian character.

In December of 1989 Carin traveled with me to Hong Kong. Brian Harper, catcher for the Minnesota Twins, and his wife Chris also made the trip. During our visit American missionary Jimmy Stewart and Chinese pastor John Tsang hosted us. Jimmy, who had played basketball at UNLV, had a great interest in outreach through athletics. John Tsang was the director of a youth camp near Hong Kong. Clinics were held at the international school in Hong Kong and at the camp.

Missionary Jimmy Stewart, Tom Roy, Brian Harper, and coach from Hong Kong

There was an air of tension in the city. Hong Kong was under British protection but would soon be returned to Chinese control. There was a sense of uncertainty among the people, many of whom had fled Communist China. Would they lose their homes, their businesses, their freedom?

Would foreign businesses pull out of Hong Kong? All of this unrest led to an openness to the gospel. It was a great time to be there.

Hong Kong is a crowded and exotic city, with a mixture of luxury and poverty. Many public bathrooms had what some call "squatty potties," a drain in the floor with steel footplates on either side. At the popular Stanley Market the restrooms had a cement floor with an open trough that had to be straddled. Water ran through the trough and emptied into the harbor.

At the other extreme is the wealth of the city. One evening an American businessman invited us to join him for dinner at an elegant restaurant on the top floor of one of Hong Kong's tallest buildings that overlooked the city's busy and colorful harbor. Chinese junks with their distinct red sails mixed with ferries and ships from around the world.

It was at that time that I had an embarrassing moment. Maybe it was the long flight to Asia or maybe it was the long days on the baseball field, but midway through the meal a muscle cramped in my leg. It hit fast and it was painful. Carin said one minute I was involved in the conversation and the next minute I was under the table.

One highlight was a day trip John arranged for us to go into Mainland China. The contrast between Hong Kong and China felt like stepping into a 1950s black and white movie. It looked like time had stopped on the other side of the border.

Jimmy accompanied us as our translator. Across the border we visited a "model city," designed for tourists. We were taken to a school for the children of government officials. The children had prepared a special Christmas program of songs and dances. They were beautiful in their colorful costumes. After they finished they wanted to hear some American songs so we sang a few Christmas carols and then "Jesus Loves Me." When Jimmy translated the words into Chinese for them they asked, "Who is Jesus?" They had never heard of Him. With the permission of the teacher, we were able to share with these children the Christmas story and the reason Jesus came to earth.

UPI team speaks to students at a private school in China.

The following are a few comments from that trip:

Having Unlimited Potential here in Hong Kong has been a real blessing for us. It's opened up some key doors for us for ministry opportunities. Those doors will give us more opportunity to be able to minister the gospel to the nation, especially at a time when it is about ready to experience a great, in many people's minds, disaster, and that is that Hong Kong will be taken over by Communist China in 1997. One thing I would like to mention about Unlimited Potential is the whole attitude that they come here with. It was very evident to the community here in Hong Kong that they came to serve. It was a very effective ministry.

Jimmy Stewart, missionary to Hong Kong

I really got excited seeing Tom Roy and Brian Harper come to Hong Kong. We thank God for you people coming; we would love to have you come back again. I really see that you people have made a very special impact on Hong Kong. I think God is doing something unique, using unique people with special talents, and we are to use it greatly for the Lord, and to do it

A baseball demonstration to students in China

while there is time. Here in Hong Kong, in nine years, China is going to take over, and now people are very receptive to the gospel, and they are more open, especially to you American people, who come with a smile, a warm heart, a special sport, and talents. I feel happy that I can be part of you.

John Tsang, Chinese pastor and camp director

Well, I can't really say in a few words an overview, but I can just say that it was the time of my life. I can definitely say that it's the most fascinating 10 days of my entire life. It was happy, sad, beautiful, ugly, exciting, boring, and fantastic. It was everything that could have possibly been packed into one week. I think this whole trip was really a trip of faith and I really feel like the Lord just brought me along and was patient with me. He taught me so many things and stretched my faith beyond what I could have ever imagined.

Chris Harper

Doors were opening to the ministry of UPI in the US and around the globe. Our first trip to Egypt was in 1990. Joel Davis and I met Jim Duffin in Cairo. Jim had been with us in Russia and this time his son Cully was with him.

Tom Roy and Joel Davis in Egypt

Jim and his son were to go to Alexandria while Joel Davis and I taught in a small village just outside of Cairo. To get Jim and his son to the station to meet their express train, we tied their luggage on top of a taxi and headed through rush hour traffic. The cab driver wove through traffic, driving over curbs and on sidewalks to get there. We untied the luggage and ran to the tracks in time to see the caboose heading out of the station. Rushing back to the cab, we tied the luggage back on, and sped to the next station. We threw their bags onto the train as it pulled out of the station, helped them jump on the moving train, and watched them wave from the car crowded with people, luggage, and chickens. As we left the station, we walked past a snake charmer. Was this a UPI trip or an Indiana Jones movie?

Joel and I were taken to a small Christian camp outside of Cairo, and we were each given 25 young men to work with, ages 16 to 25, who had been handpicked by their churches. They were Christians in a country where Christians are a small minority. For the next week we taught baseball each day and conducted Bible studies in the evenings. Much like in Uganda, we had to start from scratch when teaching baseball. We had to show them what a baseball bat looks like, how the field is laid out and how the game is played. It

Teaching baseball in Uganda

was a challenge. We trust the Lord used us to encourage those young men in their faith and that they were able to use their new skills in baseball to reach out to others in their culture.

Toward the end of the trip all of us were excited to see the pyramids at night. Although we had seen the pyramids and the sphinx during the day we were told the evening light show was spectacular. It was a sight I never got to see. I became very ill and was down for another two days with a fever of 104°. I'm guessing it was "Pharaoh's revenge." I was so ill the Egyptian doctor would not allow me to leave the country. Joel Davis probably had his greatest ministry on that trip with me as he expressed his love for Jesus by caring for me while I was sick. I am indebted to Joel. Fortunately the fever broke in time for me to make my flight home. It was an experience I will never forget.

Another unforgettable experience was going to Uganda with Russ Carr in 1989. Russ is a legend in California college soccer. When he retired from coaching, he founded a ministry called Sports Outreach Institute. Its approach was to identify one country and pour all they had into soccer ministry. Uganda was that country. Russ invited me to go with him after discussing with the Ugandan authorities that I could introduce the country to a new sport, baseball. Russ did the groundwork and our initial contact was with Barnabas Mwesinga, the Minister of Sports for the government of Uganda. Uganda was just beginning to recover from the brutal regime of Idi Amin. There were many orphans and the new government wanted to add more sports programs to help with youth morale.

When we landed, we were picked up by Barnabas who had been a national soccer champion and later coached the national team. He was a very kind and gracious man, but at the time he was not a Christian.

One of Uganda's sports is cricket, similar to baseball but with a totally different throwing technique. Barnabas was an outstanding athlete but had never played baseball, and I remember teaching him how to throw and hit a baseball. Later Barnabas became a believer in Christ and desired to use sports for outreach in his country. Eventually he became an associate of UPI and Sports Outreach Institute, teaching both soccer and baseball to the youth of Uganda and sharing the message of Christ.

In April 1990 we brought Barnabas to the United States to observe baseball in person. He was attempting to teach baseball, but he had never seen a game. This was his first time in the U.S. and he arrived with one small duffle bag. Later I learned the bag was filled with books–he did not have a change of clothes.

During his visit, we spent time in Bible study and prayer as well as many hours of baseball. We visited high school practices, watched college games, and saw the Chicago Cubs play at Wrigley Field. We also traveled together to the International Sports Coalition meetings in Dallas, Texas. It was there that Barnabas was challenged by other athletes to share his faith through sports.

While we were in Dallas, a local church sponsored a 5K race to raise interest in sports ministry. Barnabas, still a fine athlete in his forties, asked if I would take him to the race. Since I was speaking in a session that morning I couldn't take him but was able to find him a ride. I did my workshop and returned to the hotel. Just before lunch Barnabas walked into the foyer of the hotel carrying an armload of t-shirts. I asked him about the race and he humbly said it went fine.

Later I learned that Barnabas not only ran in the race and finished 15th out of 300, but he ran it in his street clothes and dress shoes–it was all he had. No one had told him about accepted running apparel. I was told that when he finished the race people at the finish line were so amazed they gave him their t-shirts.

Probably the greatest ministry Barnabas had was with me. He was eager to learn more about Christ and he spent hours in the Word. Barnabas brought great perspective to all of us in UPI, challenging us as Americans to be strong as we serve Christ because the rest of the world is looking to us as an example. We were humbled when he told us he prayed for Americans because having so much makes it difficult for us to depend on God.

It's Great to be alive because God is in control!

Action points

- Record the times God provided for you in a special way.
- How do you respond when finances are low?
- How can we all empathize more with a world that has needs?

11

Cash Money

We make many acquaintances in life but few true friends. One of my true friends is Tim Cash, who joined the staff of UPI in 1989. This was a defining moment in the history of the ministry, adding a newly retired player to the staff. Here was a man with a passion for ministry with professional baseball.

Tim Cash was born December 11, 1962, in Newnan, Georgia, to Earl and Glenda Cash. His dad, "Big Earl," started hanging sheet rock at the age of fifteen. Tim describes his journey.

> When I look back over my early days, I remember a hard-working dad and a dependable stay-at-home mom. Good parents, man! I felt very loved, cared for, and validated. I felt that I had worth as a young kid just because of feeling total acceptance and love for my siblings and me.
>
> My dad was twenty when I was born. Mom had just turned 21. I graduated from high school when my dad was 37 or 38, so we grew up with young parents. My dad was very involved in my life as far as my sports activities. He never got to play himself, so he may have lived out some of his unmet passions through me. We had an incredible bond. We played baseball and basketball, which were our two major sports. We chased them big-time.
>
> As I look back during those years, I think one of the most memorable things for me was my dad's care for the forgotten, down-and-out kids that didn't have much. We grew up

in a town that was about 75 percent white, but it was always kind of unique that about 75 percent of our team were kids from African-American backgrounds. We would go through the projects and pick up these boys. They were great little athletes, man. But those kids didn't have a dad, and my dad would take care of them. Even though we didn't have much, we had a lot of love and care. There was always food on the table to feed whoever came.

I was a white kid, but I didn't grow up with just a "white" mind-set because of the way Mom and Dad would treat all those kids out there. Also, being involved in construction work, Dad had a lot of affiliation with people from a variety of ethnic backgrounds. I had some really cool times growing up.

I graduated from high school when I was 17 years old and was much younger than the other guys. I started my senior year when I was 16, and there were seniors on the football team who were 18 and 19 at the time. It was kind of interesting going out to play against others that were a lot bigger and stronger than I was.

In football those guys ran all over me. But baseball was something I could pursue. So was hoops—I could shoot a little bit. I had a strong arm and could always hold my own in regard to my arm strength and was able to compete off the mound.

What I remember about high school was that it was a tough time. Alcohol, drugs, and all the sexual conversations were being introduced. They were being elevated and paraded around. But it's not that I had any conversations or long-term relationships with the guys I hung with. You know how at times, even hanging out and playing in sports, you still feel like an island. That's what I remember about high school.

I do remember a moment just before I started high school, being introduced to the gospel. I don't know if it was the "good news" or not, but it was a form of the gospel. A guy shared the "Romans Road" and asked me if I were to die, did I know where I would spend eternity? Shortly after that, I shared a prayer with him and started going to a church that emphasized the style of your hair, music, and what kind of movies you watched, no mixed swimming, etc. They made sure you read only the King James Version of the Bible. I didn't last very long in that, but that was the first introduction I had to the gospel—occasionally attending church but never having any root system.

I started college at DeKalb Community College in Atlanta. I played two years and got a lot of my basic college requirements behind me. It was interesting going to school, but I didn't have a high SAT score, and neither of my parents had ever attended college. In fact, no one on my dad's side of the family graduated from high school. So this was kind of a "pioneer" move in which God was allowing me to participate. From there, I attended Troy State University, and after my senior year, I signed with the Houston Astros.

The baseball was fine. I played five years professionally–four with the Astros and one with the Dodgers. I never made it past Triple A. Most of my career was spent at the Double A level, but it was a fun pursuit. It got to where I could really excel on the mound in 1986. I had a strong arm and threw the ball extremely well. But after three major arm surgeries, I was pretty much forced to exit the game as a player.

It was during that time of professional baseball in1984 when I came back from playing my first year in Auburn, New York, with the Auburn Astros in the NW Penn League that my dad sat down with me and shared with me how he had surrendered his life to Christ and was now following Jesus. Church was never a big part of our lives growing up, other than the occasional Easter or Christmas program. We never read the Word, had family devotions, or prayed—none of that stuff. But when my dad came to faith in Christ, we all saw a radical change in his life. I really admired the passion my dad had to honor God. He and Mom started going to church, and I could see there really was something alive in their lives. That was so amazing to me.

I continued to party and run; the thrill of a chase was a part of my journey then. But just before I went back to playing ball in 1985, my best buddy I grew up with came to faith in Christ and began to share what God was doing in his life. I encountered some pretty cool guys along the path that really did have an authentic walk, even though I didn't understand it.

At the end of 1985 I had my first elbow surgery. It was then that I began to contemplate and ask what was life all about? I had to come to grips with my life, my baseball career, who I was, and where I was going.

1985 is when I really got on my face before the Lord and asked Jesus to take over and become Lord and Master of my life through faith. With true repentance from my sin, I really embraced Jesus.

About that time a guy by the name of Walter Smith, who is still is a friend of mine, was crucial in my early transformation and growth. A lot of people have said when I prayed that prayer at the age of 13 I was saved. I think that was a prayer of guilt, not wanting to go to hell. In 1985, when I was 22, I prayed with sincerity.

Walter came alongside and began to disciple me and really help me in the Word. He helped me with prayer and was really just a crucial friend, kind of like a Paul/Timothy relationship right out of the gate for me. I will forever be grateful to God who brought such a guy in my life. He is a friend and a brother who cared so much more about my spiritual journey. He didn't care that I played baseball; he just cared that I really wanted to know God and honor Him. That was very, very crucial in my development.

When I went back to play in 1986, I was probably as strong as I had ever been. I was alcohol and party free. I met a lot of guys in spring training like Craig Reynolds, Glenn Davis, and a bunch of other guys who had a solid walk with the Lord at that time. Another player, Jeff Calhoun, a left-handed pitcher with the Astros, was very gracious and kind to me.

It was at that time that Jeff and his wife, Shelley, paid for me to go to a PAO conference that was to take place in November of 1986. We had won the Southern League championship that year, and I had a ton of saves. It was a great year pitching. That was fun. But the thing that was kind of cool was my spiritual development over that year and being able to share the gospel and be a part of the Bible studies with guys on the team. When the season ended, I went to that PAO Conference. That is where my eyes were opened even more to the body of Christ and the possibilities of the whole Christian journey and ministry.

I will never forget Josh McDowell. I had never heard of him to that point in my life, but he was one of the keynote speakers. Larry Burkett talked about finances, and John Trent and Gary Smalley were talking relational stuff. Those guys were some of the big-name guys at that time who were doing the big-time apologetics.

It was at that conference that I met Tom Roy and his wife, Carin. We began to connect and do so even to this day. That was such a cool thing.

Tim was showing serious interest in becoming a member of the UPI family. I remember it was a cold, icy, gray Indiana winter day when a beaten-down silver 1982 Mazda pickup truck pulled into Warsaw, Indiana. Tim Cash had made the journey from Newnan, Georgia, in his faithful truck. I was excited that he had come to see the operation, but did not want to oversell the ministry to him. After all, I had been a one-man show. We had only recently hired a secretary. I wanted to make sure that God wanted Tim with us and that it was not just me, taking a warm body to work.

We had a great time and bonded quickly. The weather couldn't have been worse for a man from Georgia. He wasn't likely to be impressed with the Disney wall art in the office. In fact, there really wasn't much in Warsaw that could compare to Atlanta. I tried to stay as neutral as I could with Tim, yet all the time praying and asking God, "Is this one you have chosen for this work?"

Tim remembers it this way:

Tom was a sort of one-man show at the time, but I really felt a burden to check out UPI. When I left Indiana after being with Tom, there wasn't much about Warsaw that was attractive. It was cold; there was ice, snow, and frigid conditions in January 1989. Yet on my way back to Atlanta, I really felt compelled in my heart, based on what God was showing me, that it was time to step out in faith and leave playing baseball behind. It was time to really follow the Lord. So in 1989 I moved to Indiana. I thought Tom was probably thinking, "What is this all about?" It was a beautiful time to see God working in my life.

There was another element to Tim's move to ministry. Tim recalled,

A few years earlier Glenn Davis invited me to go on a mission trip to Korea. He told me he would pay for me to go, and he wanted me to have that shared experience with him. The Korea team that year was made up of Tom, Glenn Davis, Jose Alvarez, Jeff Hearon, and me. I had just had shoulder surgery and was not able to do much on the baseball side. But what a transforming time that was in my journey to be exposed to missions. I saw different cultures as we stopped first in Hawaii and then throughout Korea. We visited orphanages, high schools, churches, different military bases, and other venues and saw how God was going to use that.

Tim attended our February board meeting to give his testimony and was added to the staff on a part-time basis. Tim finished his education as a full-time student at Grace College. He worked part time at UPI for $400 a month while he was in school. He received $800 a month for the summer hours of work. His main responsibilities

UPI staff: Dawn, Tim Cash, Carin and Tom Roy, Phil Menzie, Marlyn French

Early on in UPI it was just Tim Cash and Tom Roy.

at UPI then were to expand minor league contacts and to help with camps, clinics, and speaking.

That proved to be one of the greatest decisions UPI has made. Tim had the anointing of God all over him. He grew in leaps and bounds as a student at Grace, and God's favor was all over him. It was a blast to invest time into his life. He was a diamond in the rough. A diamond with Unlimited Potential.

Tim graduated from Grace College in June of 1990 and became the second full-time staff member with UPI. The decision to take on another staff member was an exciting step of faith for us. It meant taking on the responsibility for another life. It was shortly after Tim came on staff that he married Barb Ligertwood. As Barb now states it:

Tim and I met through a mutual friend and actually had a long-distance phone courtship. We met and married in five months but were only actually in each other's presence for about three weeks before we got married. Many years and five children later, I could not be more thankful for the way the Lord brought us together. Tim was already in full-time ministry when we met. About a year before that, though, I knew beyond a shadow of a doubt that the Lord had called *me* to full-time ministry. Upon meeting Tim and learning what he did, it was just more confirmation from the Lord that this was the man for me.

On December 1, 1990, I was privileged to perform their marriage in Nashville, Tennessee. Prior to that, they came to me for pre-marital counseling. It was a three-session process and a very honest time. I hope this time was valuable to them, but it also gave me time to get to know Barb. We talked about the seriousness of the wedding vows and how marriage needs to be built on truth and trust. I would present materials and then leave the room to give them time to discuss the topics alone. Finance, faith, and intimacy.

I remember the sex talk well. As the two of them came into my office, we all knew what the topic would be. After some small talk we began the session with prayer. As I lifted my head after prayer, I looked at them and said, "Tonight we are going to talk about sex. I am going to leave the room, and the first thing I want each of you to do is take off your clothes." Needless to say, their eyes grew big. Then I told them I would return in five minutes, and if they were still sitting in their chairs, we were going to have a long talk. I got up to leave and then turned around and returned to my chair. When Barb realized I was joking, she relaxed and laughed. It was her first close-up look at the real Tom Roy.

Together Tim and I traveled to clubs to speak at banquets, visit players, and conduct clinics and camps. I immediately put him to work as an instructor. The kids loved Tim and his down-home approach to life. Tim was young and uniquely gifted.

Tim grew into a very skilled student of the Word. He was always reading and asking questions. When he disagreed, he would do more research, ask more questions, and seek out others' counsel. His passion to learn the Word was a part of his gift mix. He could teach baseball, but he had a greater love of learning and teaching God's Word. A good teacher first has to be a good learner and that is something Tim has always been.

It made sense for Tim eventually to move back to the Atlanta area where he began a ministry of teaching the Bible and showing men and women how to apply it in their lives. Tim has a heart for the "down and outer" as well as the "up and successful."

Tim and I have had great days together laughing, reading, studying, challenging, planning, and praying. Tim has a passion to make Jesus real to the athlete. He has a way of putting biblical truths into language that makes men relate. His personality is larger than life and he has an insatiable hunger to learn and pass it on. Today Tim is the face of UPI to the players, and in 2008 he took over the responsibilities of executive director.

It's Great to be alive because God is in control!

The Tim Cash family

Action Points

- Name significant people God has brought into your life.

- Who are the people in your life who motivate, encourage, and help to mold you?

Chris Singelton shares at a UPI clinic in Atlanta.

(top) Tim Cash and Tom Roy with players in Milwaukee Brewers locker room
(bottom) John Smoltz shares Jesus at a UPI clinic in Atlanta.

12

To Russia with Glove

"Please fasten your seat belts. We are about to land in Moscow," was the good word from the Russian flight attendant. It had been a long flight and every baseball player was tired and hungry, yet eager. This was an historic trip. Five major league baseball players and two missionaries were flying with me into Russia in January 1990. Two months earlier when the Berlin Wall fell, the Communist empire began to crumble. The Iron Curtain had cracked open, and the first team of current major league players ever allowed into that country was about to see a world much different from the one they had just departed, the good ole USA.

The team consisted of Don Gordon, pitcher, Cleveland Indians; Jeff Hearon, catcher, Blue Jays; Danny Shaeffer, catcher, Colorado Rockies; Brad Havens, LHP, LA Dodgers; Paul Noce, second baseman, Chicago Cubs, and me. Also with us were two AIA staff members, Jim and Larissa Duffin from Canada. Larissa spoke Russian and became our set of ears during the translation by the Russian interpreter. We had no idea how this trip would provide an opening for Christ in the world of Russian athletics.

Our eyelids felt like sandpaper as we walked off the plane, but it was exciting to realize we were in Communist territory. Setting up the details of the trip had been a long and tedious process, as neither country trusted the other. We needed an official invitation from the government in Russia, which then needed approval by the U.S. government. Once we had secured the officially approved invitation, letters were sent to major league players asking them to pray about a trip into the U.S.S.R. Not many Americans had been allowed behind the Iron Curtain. We wondered how we would be received and what we would experience.

When we arrived at Moscow International Airport, Vadim, our translator, greeted us. He was a sergeant in the Red Army. With him were a few dignitaries from the Soviet Baseball Association. Baseball was not a major sport in Russia, but it was one that the Soviets very much wanted to master, much like they had done with hockey a few years earlier. Our bags and our bodies were packed into small vehicles and taken to our lodging, the Moscow Sport Hotel. This hotel was also housing all the winter Olympic athletes for the U.S.S.R.

The hotel rooms were rustic. Brad Havens and I shared a room with two single beds, worn carpeting, and a tiny bathroom with a sink and a toilet. It was January in Moscow, and the room seemed colder than the outside temperature. That first night we slept in several layers of clothing in an attempt to stay warm. It was a cold start, but the reception with the Soviet team the next day was much warmer.

UPI team at Moscow State University: Tom Roy, Don Gordon, Vadim (translator), Paul Noce, Danny Schaeffer, Brad Havens

Our time in Moscow consisted of teaching baseball clinics and visiting various sites around the city. Each baseball clinic was held in a gymnasium, since the weather prohibited teaching outdoors. Netting had been placed around the gyms so batting, throwing, and pitching could be taught indoors. For the clinics, the American pro players set up teaching stations around the gym. The Russian players were divided by the position they played and sent to different stations. Instruction lasted about two hours each day. The first clinic was held at Moscow State University.

Our first impression of Moscow was the lack of color in the city. There were long rows of gray buildings that were government housing. There was an overall look of deterioration. The government was in a state of turmoil, and the economy was suffering. One day we were taken to a store, a large building, with almost nothing on the shelves. We noticed a long line of people out the door and around the block. Suddenly a small wooden window opened, and each person in line was given something wrapped in white paper. It was a slab of ice

Trading Bible and baseball gear with Russian players

cream. It would not have been our first choice of food, especially in January, but they took what they could get. To be Russian in 1990 was tough.

We were taken to the flea market. It was a long row of small structures, most selling handmade items like dolls, scarves, knit hats, dishtowels, and knick-knacks. The snow was piled high around the shops, making shopping difficult. The people all seemed to be dressed for the weather, but it was no fashion show. The clothing was gray, brown, and drab.

The Russian baseball players we met had a keen interest in getting to know American athletes, and they were full of questions about life in the United States. They were eager to trade for American blue jeans and other American goods. We enjoyed the casual time with the players and traded our "stuff" for Russian army watches, and other items with the USSR logo.

One of the greatest memories of our time in Moscow was when the pros stood in front of the team at Moscow State University and shared their life stories. Under communist rule it was not common for someone to speak about Jesus. Later we learned that many of the Russian players had no idea who Jesus was. We were struck with the fact that we were speaking openly about our faith at a university in a communist country while we were not permitted to speak openly about Christ in public schools in America, the land of the free.

Paul Noce recalls, "One player pulled me aside, asking about how to come to know Jesus. He wanted to go to another room because he feared what might happen to him. The ministry team gathered around him to pray and encourage him."

After a few days in Moscow, I asked Don Gordon to share his testimony and the plan of salvation with the Russian team. All the American pros had Christian literature in brown paper covering ready to hand to any athlete who was interested. Larissa listened intently to make sure the translation was accurate. We prayed as Don spoke very openly and boldly about how Christ had changed his life. At the conclusion he invited any of the Soviet players who were interested in learning more about Jesus to ask us for a piece of literature that would explain this in more detail, and in Russian. As he finished speaking and Vadim translated, the Russian coach went ballistic. He began screaming at our translator in Russian. Vadim responded very calmly.

Later Larissa told us the Russian coach was very upset that we were talking about Jesus with the team. He was yelling at Vadim that this was illegal in their country and that we must stop. Vadim told the coach that he had been with us for several days and knew that we were good people. Then he added that the government was going to come down within the year anyway. For a sergeant in the Red Army, this was quite a statement. Meanwhile, as the two men argued, every one of the Russian players came up to get one of the brown paper-covered tracts.

Vadim and the coach argued a little longer before they settled down. After that, my strategy changed at the clinics. Instead of teaching, I stayed with the coach, asking him baseball questions and keeping him away from the players. This allowed the Russian players to ask questions about more than baseball; they could ask freely about Jesus.

The coach and I became better friends in the next few days. By the end of the week we had exchanged gifts. I had given him a UPI

Danny Schaeffer and Don Gordon with Russian soldiers

shirt, and in return he took the shirt off his back (sweat and all) and gave it to me. According to a translator, this coach trusted Christ the following year.

We had many opportunities to talk in depth with the players about faith in Christ. We did not know if there would be any negative consequences for them, and we wondered if there would be any spiritual fruit from that trip.

We found out, a few years later, that God had been doing a work in these men. Multi-millionaire Ted Turner had the idea of starting the Goodwill Games, an event held during the off Olympic years. The first event was to be held in Seattle, Washington, and the Russian baseball team was invited. It was during this time that I received a phone call from an AIA worker. He told me of his ministry at the games and a conversation he had had with a Russian baseball player over lunch.

When the AIA missionary turned the discussion to Jesus, the Russian baseball player stopped him and told him that he already had a personal faith in Jesus. He said a group of professional baseball players had visited his team and given him some literature. He pulled out the booklet with the brown cover and a small Bible we had given him during our first trip to Russia. His Bible was well worn, according to the AIA worker, and he said the young Russian had committed many Bible verses to memory. What an encouragement that was to all of us.

Our second trip to Russia included Danny Shaeffer and Roger Mason, both with the Pittsburgh Pirates; Todd Thomas, a scout with the San Francisco Giants; Bob Burton, a trainer with the New York Mets; Don Gordon, who was then with the Milwaukee Brewers; and me. Also joining us was Robert Lehn, a pastor who was to be our Bible teacher on the trip. It was Robert's first international experience, and unfortunately, his flight was delayed. In fact, it was delayed so long we assumed he had not made the trip. Moscow in those days was not very visitor-friendly and Robert had no way to contact us when he finally did arrive.

A few days after Robert was to arrive, the team stopped briefly at Moscow State University to look at the baseball field. (Actually, the truth is, we stopped to use the bathroom.) While we were there, a phone call came in to the university. It was Robert calling from the airport. He had been stranded at the Moscow airport for 36 hours and had been trying to contact us. If we had not stopped for a bathroom break, Robert would not have been able to reach us. Praise God for His perfect timing.

At the first clinic that day, Max, a Russian ballplayer, said his life had changed since he had asked Jesus into his heart as a result of our first visit to Russia. Max told us he reads his Bible often, and it was an encouragement to us to witness his genuine faith and his excitement in Christ. Nick, a first baseman for the Moscow State University team, came up with a big smile and recited John 3:16, in Russian of course. Nick had also invited Jesus Christ into his life during our first trip.

During the trip twenty Russian players of different ages prayed to receive Christ as their Savior. However, numbers can be deceiving. One player named Vladimir, who had been very enthusiastic about Jesus the year before, was not walking with the Lord. When we asked him about his relationship with Christ, he said it was okay. When we asked if he knew that he was a Christian he said yes, because his mother and father were Christians. Vladimir needed to be discipled.

A highlight of this trip was the opportunity to give away more than a thousand Russian Bibles. We also handed out thousands of Christian tracts on trains and sidewalks, at the Russian circus, and even at a hockey game. At one point during the hockey game, we looked around and almost everyone was reading the tract instead of watching the game.

We praise God for the open door into Russia. This is what UPI is all about—professional baseball players giving their time and talent to teach the game of baseball and share the story of Jesus Christ.

It's Great to be alive because God is in control!

Action Points

- How would you handle yourself if you were Robert in an unknown, unfriendly environment?

- Would you consider praying that God would show you a country or ministry that would stretch you and make you trust Him?

- Do you get excited when given an opportunity to do something outside the normal?

Adding to the Roster

"Spectacular achievements are always preceded by unspectacular preparation" (Roger Staubach, former Dallas Cowboys quarterback).

It's exciting to be a part of what God is doing! The opportunities kept coming, the work was growing and Tim and I were being stretched. In one year, I was away from home 299 days and I was wearing down. Here is what I wrote in a 1991 newsletter:

Recently, our 1980 Mazda with over 100,000 miles needed to go in for repair. After finishing his work, our friend tried to start the engine, only to discover the battery was nearly dead. To be quite honest, after 10 years of pounding the pavement, that's how I felt in January and February—my battery needed a recharge.

With the war in the Persian Gulf there were limited travel opportunities. I was on the road a total of 40 days during the past two months. Praise God for safety! But as I began to settle into an off-the-road lifestyle, I realized my body, mind, and spirit needed a rest. Being home has been great. But, for the first time in a long while, I experienced depression and began to question my abilities and my calling. It turned out to be a positive experience, however. I was able to spend an outstanding two months in the Word, and God has given me a fresh perspective on His calling for this ministry. He continues to faithfully open doors for new opportunities. He's added wonderfully to the staff of UPI, and there is an excellent harmony among us. We are deeply indebted to God for His grace.

During this time, I realized the need for the continuous prayer of believers who read the newsletter. Although people are praying for us, perhaps there is a tendency to stop praying when Tim and I are off the road. We continue to need your prayers on a daily basis. The times in the office are as vital to the ministry as times outside the office. We praise God for those of you who pray.

The extra time with family has been exceptional. I was able to take Amy with me to New York for the Kings College tournament, and that proved to be a special time for us. Lindsay is our "Special K" and very involved in our church musical. Carin I are also excited about many areas of our personal lives. We are in the process of preparing our home for sale. Would you please pray about this? God has gifted us with so many friends, and since last June we have either been away or have had guests every week. Our desire is for a home suitable for a ministry of hospitality.

There have been several times in the ministry of UPI that I have experienced total exhaustion from the demands of the work. We knew that I needed to set aside time for rest and restoration. But new opportunities for ministry would come in and I just kept going. Before there was time to process where we had been and what had happened, I was off to another country. I found myself running on adrenaline and becoming run down. I knew it was time to look for others to share in the work of UPI.

Andy Brown, my father-in-law, had a great interest in the work of UPI. He sincerely cared about the ministry as well as our family. One day in 1988, Andy pulled me aside for a man-to-man talk. He referred to the account of Moses in Genesis 18. He showed me how Moses' father-in-law, Jethro, observed that the task was too large for Moses and wisely advised him to divide the responsibilities.

Andy applied that to my situation. He said that if I continued at the pace I was going it would take a toll on my health and my family life. I knew Andy was right and began to ask God to provide the right individuals to join the UPI staff.

In adding staff, there were several factors to consider. First, UPI is a ministry, not a business. When we add staff they become part of the UPI family. We needed to look beyond ability and availability. We needed others with a passion for this ministry.

Second, because we work with high profile athletes, we needed people who knew the game but were not attracted to the ministry because of the athletes. We needed people whose motivation was to serve the Lord.

Third, we needed to trust that God would provide financially. I felt a very real sense of personal responsibility about asking another family to step out on faith. It was one thing to trust God for the needs of my own family, but adding other families to the mix would really stretch my faith.

Naturally the biggest consideration was that these individuals needed to be God's choice, not mine. God answered my prayer and brought some amazing people into the UPI family. These people are the heart and guts of this work.

Not long after my "Jethro talk," Tim Cash had taken the leap and came on staff with UPI part time. It was a bold move but he was a bold man. Within two years he was married and working full-time. He took over the camps and clinics in the U.S. and was critical to the ministry in maintaining contact with players. We were seeing the need for someone to disciple players in the game.

Around that time Chris Bando expressed an interest in working with UPI during the off-season. Chris had been a catcher in the big leagues, mostly with the Cleveland Indians. He was moving into coaching and wanted to use the off-season to teach Bible studies in his home area of Phoenix.

Chris has a charismatic personality and a strong faith in Christ. Baseball fans might say that Chris lived in the shadow of his older brother, Sal, who played for the Oakland A's and the Milwaukee Brewers. But no one overshadowed Chris when it came to his passion for sharing Jesus and teaching the Word.

Chris became a UPI associate, and he and his wife, Mary Beth, began holding Bible studies for baseball players and their wives in their home every week. Phoenix is home to many baseball families and the studies were well attended. This eventually led to the decision to establish a UPI office in Phoenix for the purpose of ministering to the players and their families year-round.

(left) Don Gordon, (right) Glenn and Connie Johnson

In 1991 Don Gordon joined the staff of UPI. Don had been part of a UPI ministry trip to the Soviet Union in 1989. His interest in the ministry grew and in 1991 he returned to Russia and also traveled to Bangkok. I met Don when he was with the Cleveland Indians and we stayed in touch. Don was involved in team Bible studies, and it was obvious that he loved teaching God's Word. He did a great job teaching baseball and added his unique humor to the trips.

By 1992 there were five men on the UPI staff. Tim, Don and I were full time and Chris Bando and Phil Menzie were part time. Marlyn French was the office secretary but we needed a full time administrator. When Phil was asked to consider taking the position, he prayerfully declined. However, for a while he continued to serve as the bookkeeper, and Marlyn took on some of the administrative work.

The ministry continued to have loose ends and demands, and we didn't know how we could handle it all. God provided the solution and more. When God provided a full time administrator for the UPI office, he gave us a two for one deal. Glenn Johnson, a baseball coach from Kokomo, Indiana, had already been on several UPI ministry trips and he was a skilled hitting instructor. Glenn's wife, Connie, had a background in administration with a steel company in Kokomo. When I asked them both to consider becoming part of the UPI family, they didn't hesitate. Glenn and Connie left the comforts of family, friends, and home in Kokomo and moved to Warsaw to join the UPI staff in 1991.

Connie shares a little about her life:

I lived most of my life in Kokomo, where I was the middle of nine children I met my future husband, Glenn, in our senior year of high school. By that time the country had begun to recuperate from the depression and World War II.

I didn't have much contact with Christians. We were sent to church at times but we did not learn about Christ and His saving power. Since I was one of the older siblings, I was pretty much on my own from the age of 13. My parents were so busy trying to take care of their family that in order to finish high school the older five had to work and finish on our own. I started working in my first year of high school when I was thirteen, and spent very little time at home. I stayed most of the time with a sister-in-law whose husband was in Korea (during the war). My parents never questioned where I was or what I was doing.

Then I met Glenn, and we dated most of our senior year. I knew I loved him and we planned to wed as soon as we finished school. He was 17 years old and I was 18 when we married. We had no clue what a big responsibility we had taken on but found out when we became parents of a sweet baby girl 15 months later. We believed we would spend the rest of our lives together, and we celebrated 51 years of marriage before his homegoing.

The Korean War was going on at that time, and Glenn joined the U.S. Army. While in the Army, Glenn faithfully attended church, read the Word, and tried to live the life he felt God wanted him to live. I attended church when Glenn was gone because he wanted our children to be exposed to the Christian life. When he returned from active duty, we began going to church as a family. We wanted our children to know about God's love for them.

Then I realized my need to give God my life to do with as He desired. We both felt Christ loved us and had a plan for our lives. We became very active in the church, and our biggest delight was working as sponsors for the high school kids. I worked as the church secretary and really felt we were being good examples to the kids we were working with. It was a hard, but very rewarding, ministry. We still keep in contact with many of those people now.

In 1991 Glenn retired from his job of 31 years. One day a member of the Board of Directors of UPI called and offered us both ministry opportunities. Glenn was offered the opportunity to be a member of the staff as an associate, and was thrilled to go or do whatever needed to be done. I was offered the job of overseeing the administrative arm of UPI. We accepted the offer and moved to Warsaw. We have always been grateful for the opportunity to work with UPI.

Connie has been an essential and valued part of the UPI ministry, pouring her heart into her work and keeping the office in shape so we could be free to go where God called us. The following is part of a letter from another ministry, expressing the way Connie serves:

In all the years UPI has been a part of Week of Champions, Connie has always been helpful and responsive to any and all requests we have made. We do not know her personally, only by phone and fax, but you can feel her love for our Lord and her love for people. It is evident she is exactly where the Lord has called her at this point in her life, because she is a blessing to those she helps.

We're very thankful for all she does through UPI for the Week of Champions. Tell her she is invited to attend Week of Champions any year she can come; we would love to meet her personally.

Sincerely, Gary and Wanda Wetherington,
October 22, 2002.

In December of 2007 Connie had open-heart surgery. After three months of rehab she returned to work. What a strong lady. She served as my special assistant until her retirement in June of 2009.

When Glenn, Connie's husband, became a UPI associate, he was always available for camps, international trips, or wherever he was needed. The best job description for Glenn, however, was "servant." He often expressed how humbled he felt to be used by God. He was the ultimate servant soldier. It didn't matter what the job was, from driving hundreds of miles to cleaning toilets in the UPI office, Glenn would volunteer to do it, never complaining. He was a huge part of the fiber of UPI, working hard and needing no applause.

Glenn was introduced to his Savior when he worked for a farmer during the summer between his junior and senior years of high school. The family invited him to a crusade at a park in the area. It was at that crusade that Glenn realized he needed to do something more than hear about the Savior, but no one was there to help him. He married Connie immediately after graduation from high school. Believing that every man should serve his country, Glenn joined the Army in October 1956 and served for two years with the 82nd Airborne Division.

While going through a rough time in his life, Glenn began to realize he needed to turn his life over to the Lord. He mentioned this to his pastor, and later at an evangelistic meeting Glenn prayed and asked the Lord to be his Savior. God used his testimony to show others their need for Christ.

Glenn was always very interested in sports, especially baseball. I met Glenn at a college night at a local high school. He asked if UPI might be able to use him on international trips. I told him to write out his testimony and submit it to UPI, and before long Glenn was on his way to Puerto Rico, Canada, South Africa, Uganda, and other locations around the world. He was also able to travel to closed countries we cannot name for the protection of believers there.

After returning from South Africa and Uganda, I asked Glenn which of the two countries he preferred to serve as team leader. Without hesitation Glenn said Uganda. He fell in love with Uganda and Uganda fell in love with him. Barnabas Mwesiga, the UPI associate in Uganda, and Glenn met and became solid friends. Glenn could hardly wait for the Uganda trip each fall. He was called "Grandfather" in Uganda, a title of honor. He is also known as the "Father of Ugandan Baseball."

Connie wrote: "Tom Roy was a person Glenn called his friend in the fullest meaning of the word." I would say the same of Glenn. We spent many hours together talking baseball and Jesus. Glenn's death has left a huge hole in the UPI family.

There are many others involved in the work of UPI. In addition to the staff and the players, who minister at UPI clinics or join international trips, there have been coaches, pastors, businessmen, and others who have all had a part.

We met Don Dell, the father of Tim Dell, at the Okanagan Major League Baseball Camp in British Columbia. Tim had returned from the Okanagan camp as a 14-year-old, enthusiastic about his new faith. This led Don to examine the claims of Christ and he eventually gave his life to Christ. Don came to the Okanagan camp the following summer, and when he returned home he challenged his church to start a Christian baseball camp in the Vancouver area. The church got behind it and the South Delta Baseball Camp began. One hundred forty-five young people enrolled the first year. God used the camp in a mighty way for the next four years. At least two young men who attended that camp went on to sign professional baseball contracts, including Tim Dell with the Phillies and Adam Loewen with the Orioles.

UPI was privileged to conduct baseball camps through others like Rev. Don Poyser who organized a youth baseball camp at Camp Adventure in North Webster, Indiana; Vern Gulbransen and Al Johnson who began a camp in Red Deer, Alberta, Canada, and Alex Dix who organizes a camp for Europeans in Italy. We are also privileged to provide baseball camps at Camp of the Woods in Speculator, N.Y., and at Maranatha Bible Conference in Muskegon, Michigan.

Another new arena for UPI was coming alongside a current player to help conduct an outreach in his hometown. Atlee Hammaker of the San Francisco Giants organized a crusade in Knoxville, Tennessee.

"Give Thanks, Knoxville" was held in November of 1990, and Tim Cash and I were privileged to be part of the staff. Others who participated were Dave Dravecky, Glenn Davis, Brett Butler, Scott Garrelts, Gary Lavelle, Jose Alvarez and Bob Knepper. Speakers included Walt Wiley, Don Rood, Charlie Weidemier and Art Apgar. It was a great time to work with a number of current major league players as well as to share the gospel in the city of Knoxville.

A vital part of UPI has been the partnership with Baseball Chapel, under the godly direction of Vince Nauss, in ministering to baseball players. Here is how Vince became involved in baseball ministry:

> I grew up in a religious home and attended church regularly but never understood I needed a personal relationship with Jesus Christ. I began attending Baseball Chapel services in 1983 while working for the Philadelphia Phillies at the invitation of pitcher John Denny. In June of 1984, during a road trip to St. Louis, a player (Glenn Wilson) asked me if was certain I would go to heaven if I died that night. I had assumed that God would weigh all the good things I had done in my life against the bad things and that the scales would easily tip in my favor and I would earn my way into heaven. But Glenn explained to me what the Bible said about faith and works. He shared Ephesians 2:8-9 with me, "for it is by grace you have been saved, through faith—and this not from yourselves, it is the gift of God—not by works, so that no one can boast." The Lord spoke clearly to my heart with those verses. I had lived for 26 years, not understanding the grace of God, but trusting in my good works to earn His favor. That night I knelt by the bed in my hotel room and confessed I was a sinner, expressed my need for a savior, recognized that Jesus Christ paid for all my sins on the cross and asked Jesus to be my Lord and Savior. I was baptized in March 1988.
>
> God began to work in my heart in 1994 as I became more involved in ministry as a board member of Baseball

Chapel. In the spring of 1995 I left my full-time job to pursue professional dreams as a marketing consultant. Within just a few months God began to increase my desire to serve Him and as passionate as I was about wanting to succeed in my venture, it became evident that I was being called to full-time service. I began to pray about ministry positions that would match my gifts. In December 1995 the Board of Directors of Baseball Chapel believed that God had uniquely prepared me to lead this ministry and asked me to serve as President/CEO. My life verse for ministry has always been, "I glory in Christ Jesus in my service to God. I will not venture to speak of anything except what Christ has accomplished through me" (Romans 15:17-18).

Many baseball coaches have volunteered their time to participate in UPI ministry trips, men like Jake Boss, Mike Frame, Sam Riggleman, and Johnny Hunton. Johnny, at the time of this writing, is in his eighties and continues to go on mission trips. He still breaks into a run when he takes the field. He loves to share his faith in the Lord Jesus. His energy and his passion are an inspiration. Here are some of his recollections from ministry trips with UPI:

> One of the greatest experiences of my life occurred in 1988. I was at an NCAA baseball coaches' convention in Atlanta. Attending an FCA (Fellowship of Christian Athletes) meeting one evening I met Tom Roy of UPI. We quickly got acquainted, and I told him of my pro experiences in the Yankee org. and my coaching at U. of SC (Univ. of South Carolina).
>
> I made myself available to go with groups of pros/ex-pros to do baseball evangelism. I remember a first experience at a baseball clinic at UTN (Univ. of Tennessee). Participating with us were: Brett Butler, Atlee Hammaker, Dave Dravecky, Jose Alvarez, Tim Cash, Gary Lavelle, Bob Knepper, and Scott Garrelts.
>
> From then on, most all of my trips were overseas: 14 countries and 21 trips. We worked the schedules that were

Vince Nauss, Baseball Chapel president, right, with Tim & Christine Burke

arranged by missionaries. The UPI staff members received me into their fellowship and ministry with open arms of Christian love: Tom Roy, Tim Cash, Mickey Weston, Don Gordon, Bryan Hickerson and Brian Hommel.

In most all of the countries we were well received, and hundreds of youth and their parents and coaches responded to the invitation to receive Christ. Gospel tracts were readily accepted in all venues—except Italy. Only on a couple of occasions were we limited in what we could say about our Lord and Savior. In South Korea, led around by missionary Steve Bender in 2005, Mickey Weston, Tim Hullett and I were giving some baseball instructions and witnessing for Christ in an elementary school on a USA military base. After our session with kids in grades 1-3, a teacher hurried to the principal, saying that those guys were talking about Jesus. Before the session with grades 4-6 we were told not to speak about Jesus. Wow! I paid $1300 to get to Korea to share my Christ—and now this.

Well, that afternoon we went to a large private Korean high school in Pusan. The headmaster told us to go "light" on baseball, but freely give them the gospel and Jesus. What a change in my depressed being. There were 400 in attendance. We spoke to the girls and then to boys. Several hundred stood to their feet signifying that they just prayed to receive Christ. Wow! All glory and praise to God!

In 2003 Mickey, Eddie Taubensee, and I were in South Africa. At a private school session we were told not to give an invitation to receive Christ. After our presentation, two boys came up to Eddie, who had given his testimony regarding his salvation, and said to him: "How can we get saved like you did?" Eddie about fainted, but led them in receiving Christ. He was on "cloud nine" and told us that he had never before been asked how to get saved.

I have been on trips to the Dominican Republic five times. (I regret not learning Spanish.) Practically every boy that could walk had on some sort of baseball attire and was eager to participate in the clinics. Many of them exercised faith in our Savior. On the 1990 trip there, we all stayed in one house. There was great alarm when Tim Cash spotted a cockroach and a small tarantula. What a scaredy-cat he was! Missionary Bill Stothers scheduled our clinics and translated for us.

A highlight trip to Hong Kong and China in 1991 was a great experience, though we were limited regarding evangelism. It was quite a deal doing prayer and devotionals outside our living quarters in Kunming, China, in a leisurely "open-eyed" and standing fellowship circle. We figured that our rooms were bugged and did not want to be driven out of the country for Christian activities. In our group were: Tom and Amy Roy, Dwayne Hosey, Trent Weaver, Jimmy Stewart, Robert Lehn and me. At an Olympic sports practice field the Chinese players did not show up for our clinic. Someone got a soccer team practicing nearby to come over for some baseball instructions and a game. What an exciting experience, watching Tom demonstrate the "cobra," one of his pitching skills.

Missionary Bill Cashion did a great job in setting up clinics for the three trips I made to Venezuela (1989, 90, 92). With us (not all on the same trip) were: Marty Clary, Rick Leuken, Carlos Rios, Gary Eaves, and Jose Alvarez. After a clinic at a main city park, the mayor, who observed us, commented: "These guys come all the way from the USA, paying for their own transportation, to do all of this for our kids. Our church (Catholic) is doing nothing for them."

A trip to Zimbabwe in 2000 with Bryan Hickerson and Kevin Tommasini was a great experience. The clinics were arranged by "Freddie" Sorrels. After some fruitful clinics, we went to the magnificent Victoria Falls. What a sight! From there we traveled by rental car through a large game preserve. Animals blocked the road at times, but we made our way getting great views of the wild creatures. All of a sudden I yelled at our driver, Hicks: "Stop the car! I see a giant elephant!" I couldn't get a good picture through the car window, so I got out behind the car. Someone yelled: "Get back in the car! He's wiggling his ears, meaning he is ready to charge!" Well, I got my picture, and the big thing backed away, fearing my ominous presence.

Two trips to Bolivia were great. Tom Roy, Brian Hommel, and Steve Petty were in the 1999 group. Missionary Dave Strong arranged the clinics. In a game with the Bolivians, Hommel was pitching, and a guy hit one over the right field fence on him. You should have seen Brian bear down after that. I messed up my shoe going after a pop-up, stepping in a cow pile.

Mickey Weston and I were there in 2003. Missionary Marty Childers lined up the clinics for us. Our USA ambassador and the Bolivian officials were excited about our being there. Tom, did we really have some cow's udder for one meal?

In LaPaz on one trip I got a coughing spell, and at the US embassy clinic I was asked some questions. When they heard that I had experienced a four-by-pass surgery, they said, "What are you doing up here at 13,000 ft.?"

Norm Wilhelmi, a former coach, arranged for some of us to participate in one of his camps in Rimini, Italy, in 1999. His camp was for German ball players, and it was a great opportunity for witnessing to the Germans. Mike Davis and I were in that group. Another year the wives of Norm, Tom, and me went on the trip. We got in some great sightseeing in Venice among other sites. The gelato (ice cream) was outstanding in Rimini.

In 2005 Mickey Weston and I went to Japan for clinics. It was quite a struggle for me, because of a bad case of shingles. (I had plenty of pills to consume and came home addicted.) Mick put me in a separate room from him in the hotel, probably thinking my "leprosy" was catching.

Tom Roy took Brian Harper, Brian's two sons, Dave Hasiuk, and me on a trip to Taiwan in 1993. A great thrill was experienced when Brian and I were given the opportunity to give our testimonies at a gathering of about 20,000 people at a Luis Palau evangelistic crusade in a stadium. Alex Tan, of the O. C. Ministries/Sports Ambassadors, set up our schedule. Another thrill on that trip was when, after dark on a drive over a mountain, the bus driver passed a truck on an "S" curve.

Missionary Halle August, who has developed a sports complex in Nicaragua, hosted Bryan Ballard, Mickey and daughter Erica, and me in 2007. I really enjoyed the ministry and fellowship there. It surely has been great being with you and the guys in UPI service.

God was moving, not only in the USA but also around the world. A huge boost to the world of International Sports ministry was the beginning of the International Sports Coalition. Eddie Waxer was the original point man for this work. The vision God gave him to use international sports as an evangelistic tool expanded to many countries of the world. Over 150 nations are now developing ways to use sports to further the gospel of Jesus Christ in their countries. We live in exciting days!

Love in Jesus, Johnny, Phil. 1:3.

We are so thankful for all who have had a part in this ministry. What an honor to be able to work alongside these people! God provided opportunities, and then He provided His people to fill each opportunity. We have seen lives changed, both in those who served and in those who were being served.

It's Great to be alive because God is in control!

Action Points

• Have you ever overextended yourself? What have you learned about yourself after those situations?

• We each have specific gifts and talents. Who are you surrounding yourself with to help accomplish your tasks? Have you considered adding those who complement your gift?

Johnny and Patricia Hunton

152   Released

Instructional League

Pro baseball has a special classroom for top prospects in the minor leagues. It is called Instruction Ball. This is a four-to-eight week experience where players are taught and practice the finer points of baseball. It is an honor to be invited by a major league team, and very few get the chance. Some of the best instructors in baseball work with players individually to make them better, fully equipped for what they hope is ahead, a chance to play in the big leagues.

Likewise, in life, no matter what our age or experience, God often takes us through experiences where we are instructed in the finer points of intimacy with God and Christian living. Some instruction is not fun and may, in fact, be painful, but it is needed to mold us into the person He wants us to be.

Spiritual Warfare

It was Easter Sunday when I boarded the first of three flights that would take me to Sophia, Bulgaria. I had no idea, sitting in church that morning with my family, that this trip would be one of the most difficult experiences of my life. The trip had been set up several months in advance and I was excited about the invitation to visit the former Soviet satellite country.

A coach from Seattle was scheduled to go on the trip but at the last minute he had to back out. I didn't think it was necessary to cancel the trip, even though our policy as a ministry has always been to avoid traveling alone. I thought it would be fine, just this once, even though the invitation was through the baseball association in Bulgaria and I would not be working with any churches or missionary once I arrived.

I was able to catch a few hours of sleep on that flight but I noticed a scratchiness beginning in my throat. When I landed in Bulgaria, I was met by Emil Nasapov and Dimeter; both were leaders in the Bulgarian baseball association. The Sofia airport was small and had a very Eastern European look. As in Russia, the buildings all looked gray. The roads were in poor condition, most of the equipment was Russian, and the majority of cars were the Russian-made Lada.

Emil got a cab that took us to my place of lodging, "The Ademik," a dormitory-style hotel that was very similar to the Moscow Sports Hotel. My room was about 8' by 12' with a bathroom and a closet. The bathroom had a sink, a toilet, a showerhead and a drain in the floor. Towels and toilet tissue were not provided.

The room was 50 degrees, but compared to Russia it felt warm. My throat felt worse and I wondered if it was just allergies or if I was getting sick. Hopefully I would be able to sleep well that night.

After I had unpacked, I went to dinner with Emil and Dimeter. As we ate that first night I had an opportunity to share my faith with both of my hosts. Dimeter, Emil's assistant, felt he was a Christian because he was associated with the Orthodox Church. Emil did not seem to have any spiritual background. I was very thankful for the time with these two leaders and I looked forward to the rest of the week.

That first night I noticed a striking cultural difference between Bulgaria and the United States. Nodding the head up and down meant "no" and nodding side to side meant, "yes." That could be very confusing, and I would need to be careful or it could lead to some big misunderstandings.

I was in bed by 8:30, looking forward to a good sleep. Two hours later I woke up very thirsty. There was nothing to drink and I wasn't sure if the tap water was safe. I could hear laughter down the hall, so I decided to ask someone for help. Unfortunately, no one understood English. Finally someone understood "coca cola" and opened a window, pointing down the street and giving directions that I could not understand.

I went to the elevator and pushed the button for the first floor. It kept passing my floor so after about 15 minutes I finally pushed the "up" button. I got in the elevator and ended up in the basement. The hotel was dark and dreary and there was a dark haired woman dressed in dark clothing sitting behind an old desk. She spoke no English; she just pointed to the door.

I wandered out into the street but there were no streetlights and there was garbage everywhere. It felt good to get out of my room for a while as it had begun to feel closed in, but this did not seem like a safe place to be at night. I decided that the next day I would ask Emil if we could stop somewhere and get some drinks. When I returned to my room that night I thought I would pass the time by doing some floor exercises. But when I got down on the floor I saw the carpet was filthy. So instead of breathing in whatever was in that carpet, I wrote in my journal.

When you lie awake, the hours pass very slowly, especially in unfamiliar places. It was an extremely lonely time. As I lay there thinking, the Lord slowly began to impress on me the need to plan more time at home. It wasn't the first time. I remembered the kind advice of my father-in-law about dividing my responsibilities. But once again I found myself on a schedule of back-to-back trips, traveling nine to ten months out of the year. I knew the constant travel took a toll on my family and my health, but when new opportunities came in I wanted to accept them all. I sensed God was showing me now, in the loneliness of this little room in Bulgaria, that I needed time to be renewed—not just physically, but mentally, emotionally, and spiritually as well.

In the early morning hours I decided to cancel scheduled trips to France and Sweden and clear my calendar through the end of the year. God confirmed that decision with a total sense of His peace. With that in mind, I wrote a fax to be sent to the UPI office the following day. I asked them to see if the trips to Sweden and France could be rescheduled for a later date. That was a tough decision but I knew I needed to do it.

That night I wrote in my journal, "You would think I'd get used to the heartaches of leaving home, but I don't think I ever will. It really takes a certain amount of grace from God to be able to leave my family and come to this kind of place. Thank you Lord, that you have given me some peace this first evening, even though there were times that I was very lonely."

The first few days were rough. I was hit with a powerful sense of loneliness, fear and doubt. I realized I was far from home, and I really missed the people I loved. I believe it was more acute since I was there alone. The loneliness I felt gave me a much deeper understanding of those who experience loneliness all the time. I continued writing in my journal.

> I miss the convenience of talking to Carin on the phone; I've become so accustomed to it. I realize how much I miss the people I love and who love me. It was so neat to go for a walk this past weekend with Amy and hear her tell me she loves me. That really was special. It's now 3:30 in the morning and I've just had a great time of prayer. I've really been under attack and I want to get home as fast and as soon as I can. This is very humbling, and I've asked God to give me some peace in this situation. It's also been very good to get before Him in prayer and realize my need for Him in every situation. I really need to get off the road. I want to be home. My prayer is that I can make it through this trip and then spend some time re-evaluating things in my life.

I continued to write,

> At this point I believe the greatest need for the ministry of UPI is an international director, as I question my ability to continue at this pace. I think I can do it all, but I really can't. I do not want to run in the flesh, I want to run in the Holy Spirit. I need to be praying that God will bring someone to take over the international portion of the ministry. On this trip I have felt such a need to have someone with me, another believer to pray with. I feel so alone, completely alone. I can't send people out on trips like this by themselves. I feel like I am in jail, in solitary confinement, and it's brutal. I have no

one to talk with, other than the Lord, and sometimes I get so worked up it's hard even to read or pray.

I realized I should not have made that trip alone. Who was I to think I could do it?

One thing that helped me get through the long hours of loneliness was reading my Bible. It was my only companion. There was nothing else to read, and if there were, it would not have been in English. I read in my Bible about the missionary journeys of Paul and learned some things that I will never forget. One place was in Acts 16:8 where it tells of Paul's stopping in Troas near the city of Troy. There was an open door for him to minister there, but he had no peace of mind about it and left. I needed to learn that not every open door means that I have to go through it. God can accomplish His work without me. If God does not give a peace about a trip it may mean the timing isn't right yet. At a later time Paul was able to return to Troas.

On Paul's first missionary journey, recorded in Acts, he took Barnabas with him. Acts 15 talks about the church in Jerusalem sending men named Judas and Silas with him. Silas accompanied Paul on other trips. The Bible tells of many missionary trips but there were very few times where individuals traveled alone. When they did, they met with other believers when they arrived. In the book of Mark, Jesus' followers were sent out in pairs. Reading all this was a valuable reminder for me. It was imprinted on me how vital it is for us to have the support of other believers.

Once again I wrote in my journal, "I miss fellowship with other believers at this time, and my only strength has been to go to the Lord tonight. I trust that He will bring me through this. The loneliness is so deep I feel like I'm experiencing a little bit of what hell must be like. There are no other Christians here for support. I need to remember this for the future."

I didn't sleep that entire first night. Dimeter came in the morning, and we had breakfast together. By that time I had a bad cold, and he was trying to help in any way he could. Because of the cold weather, he shifted the clinic to be indoors. Before the clinic Dimeter told me that baseball had been played in Bulgaria for about six years. There were only about 10 people participating at that time. There were many others who wanted to play but because there were no gloves, bats, or baseballs it wasn't possible.

We had two good sessions in baseball that first day, and I had a couple of opportunities to share my faith. At the restaurant that night I had a very open conversation with Dimeter about Jesus. He was interested enough to ask me to come to his home one evening to share about Jesus with the entire family. Emil said also that his wife was very interested. Fortunately, they both spoke English. As we continued the conversation, I learned that the next flight out of Sophia was not until Sunday. God was just going to have to give me the grace to make it through the week. The people were treating me very well, but I still missed my family so much.

That evening back in my room I wrote in my journal:

> One of the toughest times is when I am alone. That's when I think about my family and feel helpless to take care of them. I have to trust that God will protect my family. When I keep busy, I don't have time to think about family. I wish my faith were strong enough that I did not worry about them at all. I love them a whole lot and need to spend more time with them. It's good, though, that I have really had time to spend with the Lord.

Once again I was awake all night. I believe I was wrestling with the evil one. Terrible thoughts went through my head of my family being brutally murdered, tortured, and other unthinkable things. Spiritual warfare is real. I had read about it and heard others speak of it, but now I was experiencing it. It was more than loneliness and discomfort. It was fear. It was a direct attack on my soul.

I was wishing there was something, TV, radio, or anything else to occupy my mind. Somehow I made it through the night but the lack of sleep was really getting to me. The next morning Emil told me the mayor of Sophia wanted to meet me on Friday. Because of that we would be canceling the baseball clinic. He felt this was the politically correct thing to do and would be a great benefit to Bulgarian baseball.

The baseball instruction seemed to go very well. Soon it was time to go back to my "jail cell." Again I wished I had a roommate. I wrote,

> I'm probably going to wear a hole in this carpet from my pacing back and forth praying. Well, I guess I'm stuck here for the full seven days, and I'll just have to do the best I can. I guess there is some comfort in knowing that there is no way to leave, even though that seems kind of warped. One good thing is they got me some fruit juice, so I do have something to drink. They have also told me that the water in our facility is good, and I guess I'll just trust them on that one. I sure hope it is, otherwise I'll be dealing with more than just the head cold. Today they asked me if I wanted a heater in my room because they could see I was not feeling well and it was getting colder outside. I killed my first cockroach before I got into bed. I wonder how many other critters are in here.

It was the third night and I desperately needed to sleep, but I began thinking about home. I looked at my watch and started thinking about what time it was in Indiana and wondering what my family was doing. I needed to concentrate on the week ahead and focus on what I needed to do in Bulgaria. I was almost ready to fall asleep when I killed another cockroach. This was turning into a vicious cycle of homesickness, sleeplessness, and sickness. I prayed that my system would hold up throughout the week ahead.

I wrote in my journal,

> It's 2:00 a.m. and I'm having trouble breathing because I'm so congested. I feel like I am under spiritual attack again. I have been in this kind of battle before but never alone. I have never experienced this kind of thing with such relentlessness. I feel like I'm losing it. I need to go home but the Lord is going to have to intervene. Spiritually it's been a great experience, even though it's been very difficult. I hope I can get a flight home tomorrow. I've never felt this way before, but I feel very strongly about leaving. I hope

Emil will allow me to leave before the week is over. I have such mixed emotions. I feel like such a failure, but I feel like what I am doing is very right. I pray that God will show me what I am supposed to do and that I will be able to handle whatever He has for me.

I feel such a peace about going home and yet I know that there's a very real chance that I will not be able to leave tomorrow. It's another four days until the next flight leaves but I feel like it is God's will for me to leave. This is one of the most humbling experiences I've ever been through in ministry. In twelve years of travel I have never felt like this or left in the middle of a ministry trip. I know there is a reason why I had asked for prayer from so many people back home. God has shown me on this trip that I'm not able to handle it by myself. I now realize that I need to be surrounded by believers when I travel to countries like this. It's a lesson I've had to re-learn, and I guess this is the only way God can teach me. I am embarrassed even as I write this but I need to write it down so I can read through it later and remember what I've just learned. I've never felt the kind of emotional and spiritual pressure I've had these past three days. I'll find out tomorrow if it is God's will for me to leave and if there is a flight available. I pray that since God has given me such a peace about leaving that I will pursue it, even though it will be very humbling to approach Emil and Dimeter about it. I still feel a tremendous battle inside and hope I can get some sleep.

But it didn't happen.

As I made the decision to leave, the conversation with Emil over dinner came to my mind. He had asked what was more important, serving God or family. I don't know where that came from. I responded that it was important to serve God and that He would direct you about your family. As I thought about his question and my answer, I felt like God was speaking to my own heart. I had spent the past twelve years traveling, serving God and others. The girls were growing up fast and there wasn't much time left with Amy at home. It was time for me to change my schedule and spend more time with Carin and the girls. Carin had put up with a lot with all my travel, and I felt like the conversation with Emil was confirmation that I needed to make some changes.

I also thought back to a recent conversation with Tim Cash. I had shared with him privately that I felt like I was not supposed to go to Bulgaria. I didn't know why but I just didn't feel right about it. I remember that I just kept talking so Tim wouldn't have a chance to respond. I didn't want to listen to his thoughts. Like many men, I don't put much value on feelings, but in this case I felt like Jonah. When God told him to go he went in the opposite direction. I felt like God had been directing me to spend more time with my family and I had said, "No, I've got trips planned."

It was totally humbling to be in that position, but I believe God was teaching me that working for Him was not the same as being in God's perfect will. Here is another excerpt from my journal.

> Tonight God is showing me how much He cares for me. He is showing me that He called me to this ministry and has allowed me the joy of sharing the gospel around the world. Although there have been difficult times, He has given me a better understanding of His protection and provision.
>
> Carin has kept things going at home and I feel strongly that God is saying I need to be there for her and for our girls for right now. I also need time to regain my emotional and spiritual strength. I am overwhelmed with peace at this moment as a result of giving this over to Christ. No matter what the result tomorrow, this has been a lesson that I could not have learned any other way. Although the past few days in Bulgaria have been hell for me, I realize I needed to go through this. I trust I will never forget what I learned.

It was humbling to have to learn what I had spoken to others about. Although I had been spending time each day in the Bible, I had been pursuing opportunities that seemed good to me without asking the Lord if these opportunities were in His best plans for me. A challenge

I had given many times to others was, "Don't look for what is good, look for what is best." God was using my own words to teach me.

The next morning, after much prayer, I asked Emil if there was any way I could leave early. He was very kind and without hesitation he took my ticket and sent a young man on a bicycle to see if the airlines would change my flight. It was interesting to me that Dimeter, a highly educated man from a wealthy family, said that I had made the right decision to leave. I knew that Emil and Dimeter would not understand the spiritual dynamic working in my life but they could see that I was sick, so that is the reason they thought I asked to leave. Then two things happened next to confirm my decision.

First, the young man returned from the airport. There were no flights scheduled until Sunday, but he had asked if by any chance there was a plane leaving that day. He was told that a plane had landed unexpectedly and was scheduled to take off again in a few hours. Second, the airlines exchanged my ticket without any extra charge. No one could believe it. I was told that normally any changes in flights resulted in hefty fees.

With a thankful heart I boarded the flight for the ten-hour trip to New York. I slept for eight hours and when I arrived in New York I found a hotel and called Carin. She could tell I was hurting as I told her about the four days in Bulgaria. I told her what God had shown me about the ministry, the travel, the kids and the lesson I had learned about traveling alone. I slept well that night. I was in God's will. The next morning I was able to board a flight to Fort Wayne, again without an extra charge. What a blessing!

On that flight I spent time thinking about all God was doing in my life. He had called me to Himself and He had called me into a ministry I love. He had taken me to some amazing places and allowed me to see Him work. He had brought others to work alongside me in the ministry and faithfully provided for every need. He had been incredibly patient with me and had taught me so much in His Word. But I guess some things I had to learn the hard way. I had taken a long trip to a lonely place so he could teach me that He is the One who leads and I am to follow. What would He teach me next?

UPI staff at retreat in mountains

Family Issues

Sometimes the worst times are the best times. It is not during times of ease but during difficult times that we learn. It is often in failure that we grow stronger. It is in painful situations that we become aware of how dependent we are on our God. The humbling experience in Bulgaria was a valuable lesson for me. But it was not the only difficult time for me in ministry.

UPI is a family. We are not just employees of an organization. As human beings we are built for more than work; we are built for relationship. Our Creator designed us for relationship with himself as well as with others. When those relationships are broken it is painful. Phil Menzie and Chris Bando had both been associated with UPI at one time and had moved on to other things. It was not easy but it was part of growing and following God's leading. I was aware of all this but I was still not prepared when Don Gordon resigned from UPI. It was one of the most difficult times of my life because UPI is a family and his resignation felt like a divorce.

Don and his family had joined the staff of UPI in 1992 and we had become good friends. The friendship continued when they moved to Arizona to work with players in the Phoenix area. Carin and I spent time with them each fall, meeting with players and visiting with Don and Deb into the night.

Arizona is home to a large number of professional baseball players and their families. Under Don's leadership the ministry grew. Each week there were couples' studies, men's studies and women's studies. Don met regularly with several of the men for one-on-one discipleship. There was a women's retreat in the fall and a men's retreat in the winter. Don was doing a great job of building on the ministry that Chris Bando had begun.

But Don felt overloaded by the demands of ministry. Bryan Hickerson had been active in the men's studies, and he joined the UPI staff to help relieve Don of some of the work. But Don continued to work long hours and felt burned out. Taking time off to rest did not seem to help. A retreat was planned for the staff and their wives in the mountains of Tennessee. At the retreat the Gordons shared how they felt overwhelmed and alone in Arizona. We prayed together and I assured him that I would speak with the board to see what could be done to help.

At the next UPI board meeting I presented my report and thanked the board for providing the staff retreat that included the wives. I shared with them my concern for the Gordons. I told them I had assured Don I would speak with the board to see what could be done to help. It was decided that another board member would follow up and I would not be involved. In fact, I would be put under the same microscope. I was surprised but realized it was a wise decision. The board had put much prayer into the decision. They were my authority and God was using them. I called Don to tell him about the decision of the board. I told him they would be looking into his situation but I would not be a part of the process. He seemed encouraged that at last something was happening.

The process began soon after that. The board member visited each UPI family and asked them all the same questions about relationships among the staff, my leadership style, and their concerns. After a long process of prayer and evaluation the board met again. I was excluded from the meeting. It was decided that Don would be given a sabbatical for six to nine months for the purpose of rest and restoration. I was invited back into the meeting and learned it was a unanimous decision. Board chairman Randy Swanson would be going to Arizona to inform the Gordons of the decision. I asked to accompany Randy because of my friendship with Don and Deb, and the board agreed.

Randy did a great job of humbly presenting the decision of the board. He was gentle, caring and direct. The decision included closing the UPI office in Phoenix during the sabbatical. The Gordons would receive full salary and benefits but would have no ministry responsibilities. The board had made arrangements for the Gordons to meet with a local ministry during that time to build into their lives. Randy would be staying in touch with Don, and my role would be to stay in contact with the ministry working with the Gordons in Phoenix. After a time of praying together, Randy and I returned to Indiana.

It was a painful time but it was a time of growth for me, for the staff, the board, and I believe for Don and Deb. Near the end of the six months, the board decided to extend the sabbatical for the full nine months. I was given the task of calling Don to let him know. Within a few days he called to say he was resigning.

As the reality of the Gordons' leaving sank in, I was a mess. UPI had lost a family member and Carin and I had lost a friendship. I felt like a failure and I questioned my leadership, my calling, and my ability to trust others. The board had done everything possible to resolve the issues by providing the Gordons with time to rest without the concerns of ministry. I will always be grateful for the godly leadership of the board during that time. They were men of wisdom and prayer. When the whole ordeal was over they could see the toll it had taken on me and gave me an eight-week sabbatical.

I needed a change of scenery. Carin and I spent the time at our cabin in Wisconsin where I had many hours to read, reflect, and pray. During that time I took an eight-week course on understanding thinking patterns taught by Jerry Price, author of *Twisted Thinking Transformed*. Jerry is a Christian counselor and he and I developed a deep friendship. He challenged me and helped me process some of the things I had been through. I learned much from him and was able also to gain perspective on what had happened during the past year. I learned several lessons:

1. *I need to accept responsibility.* As the leader of the ministry I was ultimately responsible for the staff and events connected to the ministry of UPI. I am thankful for the painful experience I went through and for what God taught me.

2. *I realized how much the staff cared for me.* I had been focusing so much on this one issue that I had neglected the rest of the staff. They stood by me the entire time, praying and offering support and encouragement. I will never forget that. When I felt I had failed them as well as the Gordons, they were there.

3. *I was too naive.* I took everyone at his word. As a minister I need to show compassion, but I also need to look beyond people's words to their intent. I needed to learn discernment.

4. *Things do not always work the way I imagine they will.* It was my dream that the entire UPI staff would all retire together and live happily ever after. It is a rare thing for an entire ministry staff to stay together indefinitely. Change is a part of life.

5. *Pain is a part of life.* I needed to accept that God is in control even when things don't work out the way I hope they will. My friend Chaplain Chuck Wood told me, "Pain is just weakness leaving the body."

6. *I need to be totally dependent on God.* God sometimes gives us more than we can handle to get us to look to Him.

7. *I need time to be restored.* Rest and relaxation are needed to repair a weary soul.

"Faith does not operate in the realm of the possible. There is no glory for God in that which is humanly possible. Faith begins where man's power ends" (George Mueller).

Death of a Teammate

The UPI family lost another member when our friend and co-worker Glenn Johnson suddenly went to be with the Lord. Glenn was a no-nonsense, straight shooting man's man. He wore a military "flat top" haircut even when he no longer had much hair to cut. He was willing to do any job and was happy just to be able to work. He was a hard worker and he didn't tolerate laziness or excuses. He loved teaching baseball and he loved kids.

Glenn had a daily "uniform." He would usually show up in his shorts and a t-shirt, no matter what the weather. His formal attire was a running suit. He often wore a baseball hat but always respectfully removed it when he was indoors. One of his favorite shirts was a pink collared shirt and he was quick to challenge anyone who commented on it. He told them he was "man enough" to wear pink.

One day my phone rang, and I heard Connie, Glenn's wife and our UPI administrator, say, "Tom, something is not right with Glenn." I arrived before the rescue squad and saw that Glenn was not himself. He was sitting in his blue recliner and was trying to talk but was having trouble with the words. I grabbed his shoulder and told him I loved him and help was on the way. I told him I would ask him some questions and he could just shake his head yes or no. I asked him if he knew who he was. He nodded yes. I asked if he was in any pain and he shook his head no. I could see the concern in his eyes.

When the EMT arrived the first man through the door seemed a little too jovial and I was irritated. He began to joke with Glenn and I wanted to hit him. This was my friend and the EMT guy was making light of the situation. Later I learned this is part of the procedure. One of the first signs of a stroke is the inability to smile. He was able to determine that Glenn had indeed had a stroke. By that time Glenn could barely make any sound.

They gently strapped Glenn on a cart and told him they were taking him to the hospital for testing. As we watched them take Glenn to the rescue vehicle, his eyes were wide with fear wondering what was happening. He knew something was not right.

Connie and I followed the EMT rescue vehicle to the hospital and went to the emergency room. A few friends had gathered and we prayed for wisdom for the doctors and comfort for Glenn. Connie was glad to be surrounded by friends, but she just wanted to see Glenn. After some discussion the hospital staff allowed her to see her husband. She was gone a short time and returned with fear on her face. She had seen Glenn in great pain, battling for his life.

The doctors came into the waiting area to tell us they were putting Glenn on a Flight for Life helicopter to take him to a larger hospital in Fort Wayne. We went to the car for the 50-minute drive and arrived ahead of the helicopter. We knew something was very wrong. As we learned later, Glenn had experienced a stroke and as a result a blood clot had been released, causing massive hemorrhaging in his brain. This was what was happening about the time Connie had gone in to see him. Glenn was fighting the pain. The doctors had determined that Glenn's only chance of survival, since he was fighting so hard, was to temporarily paralyze him before putting him on the helicopter.

Once Glenn was brought into the Fort Wayne hospital, the doctor examined him and came out to explain Glenn's condition. He was gentle but direct. He said Glenn had suffered a bad stroke and the chance he would survive was slim. They would do what they could to make him comfortable. Our good friend was in his final hours on earth. We were all in some level of shock, and I was thinking that just a few hours earlier I had been talking with Glenn in his home.

During the next few days there were many visitors to the hospital. We could see that God was faithfully giving strength to Connie and her family. As people came to comfort them we saw Connie and her kids, in typical Johnson style, caring for their visitors.

Finally, on the afternoon of the May 5, 2005, Connie came out from sitting beside Glenn and told us, "He isn't here anymore." She knew Glenn was no longer a patient in a hospital but a citizen of heaven. Her daughter also knew he was gone. The doctor came and did some tests and confirmed what they already knew.

The funeral home was packed. As hundreds of people came to offer comfort to Connie and her family, they told story after story of how Glenn had impacted their lives. Glenn had always been for the underdog, believing in them when no one else did. There were many tears from those telling of Glenn's giving them hope and direction.

In honor of Glenn, the UPI staff all attended the service in running suits. Each of us shared what Glenn had meant to us. When the funeral was over, I sat down and wrote God a long letter, on a short piece of paper. Glenn's life remains an example to each of us. His death was a huge loss.

Such events as the loss of ministry colleagues, whether through resignation or death, often cause us to question our plans and strategy. A paraphrase of statements by Andy Stanley is helpful here. "We need to be reminded that our vision must remain clear and stay the same, but we must understand that our plans can change…In times of uncertainty, plans fail, and when they do, we feel like failures but our vision stays the same…We may be infatuated with our plans, but we should be in love with our vision."

It is Great to be alive because God is in control!

Action Points

- How do you handle conflict in a Christian manner?

- Have you experienced the death of a loved one? How did you handle the loss?

- Have you ever experienced spiritual attack or warfare? What did you learn from it?

The Pitch Heard 'Round the World

"The measure of leadership is not the quality of the head, but the tone of the body" (Max DuPree).

Mickey Weston knelt beside the old man as he clung to his last breath in a barren Russian hospital room, and offered peace. Only minutes separated this man from eternity and he was now being ushered into the presence of God, as Mickey held his hand and gently shared the gospel of Jesus. The man could barely move, much less talk. But through the pain this unknown Russian gave his life

Mickey Weston and Mike Davis in Bangkok

to Christ and then gave up his spirit to eternity. It was a deathbed conversion for sure. At that moment I knew Mickey Weston was a special man.

Mickey was the next man to join the UPI staff. He had a heart to use the game as a platform to minister and he showed a sincere heart for people and for missions throughout his baseball career. Mickey pitched professionally for fifteen years and he and Lisa paint the picture of the life of a professional baseball player.

Here is how Mickey tells it:

I grew up in Flint, Michigan, the youngest in a family with four kids, ages five and under: Debbie, Denny, Linda and Mickey. Thirteen months separate my sister and me, thirteen months separate my sister and my brother, fifteen months separate my older brother and my older sister. We were raised for my first ten years in Flint, Michigan. As I was growing up I was interested in all sports. If you wanted to find me, you would have to come outside. We didn't have an Atari—not many kids did—so we were outside playing all the time. I was not a great student at the time, as my report cards showed.

When I was ten, we moved from Flint out into the suburbs, which was a great move for me because it got me out of the city into a little safer environment. I really began to excel in baseball, and at the age of eleven made my first all-star team. From that point on I developed a love for football and I also played basketball, basically to stay in shape until baseball season.

I did not grow up in a family that sought after God. We seldom went to church, maybe only on Easter or Christmas, and God was not honored in the home. As I entered my teen years, I really felt there was something missing in my life. By junior high my studies had begun to kick in and I began to excel in the classroom, being in the top ten in my class my first two years of high school, and becoming a National Honor Society student in my junior year. When I got into high school I became more popular because I was a good athlete. But as I began to excel on the baseball and football field and in the classroom, I really began to sense that something wasn't quite right in my life.

At the age of sixteen I remember going out in the middle of a field and crying out to God, wanting to know who I was and who He was. I began to go to church on my own but the church I attended did not teach the gospel. They spoke about good works getting you into heaven but I still knew there was something about this Jesus. I continued to go to church every Sunday. In an effort to gain others' acceptance, I would do just about anything. That led me down some paths that I'm not proud of today.

I went to Eastern Michigan University on a partial academic scholarship and felt like that was going to be my stage to let the world know who Mickey Weston is. Eastern had an excellent baseball program but I did not get an athletic scholarship. I had to try out for the team in the fall and thought that I was going to show the coaches who I was, not realizing that Eastern recruited from five different states. At the end of the fall I was the last pitcher out of fifteen to be chosen. I realized at that point that only the top ten really have an opportunity to pitch during the season. I had a lot of work to do during that off-season.

It was at that time that my eyes began to open to the reality that at any time I could lose my athletics, my studies, and my relationships. Then God sent Dave Booram with Campus Crusade for Christ to speak to our baseball team. He brought with him an Eastern Michigan University swimmer who shared his testimony about how he had tried everything to fill the void in his life and didn't find anything lasting until he entered into a relationship with Christ. As he shared, my heart began to race and I realized this was what I really wanted.

So on Friday afternoon, February 15, Dave Booram came to my dorm room and began to present the gospel to me through a booklet called the "Four Spiritual Laws." Then he asked me two questions, "If I were to die right then, would I go to heaven or to hell?" I told him I would go to heaven because I didn't want to go to hell. Then he asked me the next question that really got me thinking. He said, "Why should God let you into heaven?" I listed several things I thought would show that I was a good person. Then he shared with me Ephesians 2:8-9, which says, "For it is by grace you have been saved through faith—and that not from yourselves; it is the gift of God—not by works, so that no one can boast."

I bowed my head and said a simple prayer and asked Jesus to save me. David Booram met with me for personal discipleship and showed me how to share my faith. I began to be involved in the weekly meetings of Campus Crusade for Chris and eventually became the leader in my junior year.

I began to excel on the baseball field. Shortly after I accepted Christ, I was able to make the spring trip, which was my first answer to prayer. The only reason I made it was that one of our top pitchers had not been going to class and the coach had said that he would leave anybody home that was not attending classes. So on every list I saw, that pitcher's name was scratched out and my name was written in. I really saw the hand of God in that right away.

Over the course of the next two years I gained ten miles an hour on my fast ball and went to being #15 to #10 and to #1 in my junior year with Eastern Michigan's baseball team. As a junior I was named to the all-regional tournament team. After defeating Florida State in one game and Oklahoma in another, I was drafted by the New York Mets in the 12th round in June of 1982, the same year the Mets drafted Dwight Gooden, Roger Clemens, Randy Myers, Floyd Gillman and traded for Ron Darling and Ray Hernandez, who all became solid major leaguers.

In 1982 I began my career in professional baseball with the New York Mets, slowly moving up the ladder through the system. In 1983, in the middle of my senior year, I married Lisa, and we began what we call "our career" together in professional baseball. Throughout our career in the game we held Bible studies for players and wives. We had a passion for Christ and for others to come to know Him. We really thought of ourselves as missionaries in the game of baseball. I was still very young in my faith, but Lisa had grown up in the church.

I did not have outstanding physical abilities on the field compared to many of the players that were drafted, but I continued to put up solid years in the minor leagues and was one of those guys they liked to have on the team as having a stabilizing influence. I really believe that is what kept me in the game. The Mets had a "log jam" in pitching throughout their system, so moving up the ladder was slow. I spent three years in Double A and really felt like my last year in Double A in 1988 was probably going to be my last year in professional baseball.

Lisa and I had made plans back when I was playing in A ball in 1985 for me to go to grad school. I was accepted in an exclusive Christian counseling program in Atlanta, Georgia, called Psychological Studies Institute in conjunction with Georgia State University. I would get a Masters in psychology from Georgia State, and would get a special diploma from PSI. After talking with the faculty of PSI, they encouraged me to wait until I was finished playing baseball before I pursued my education. We felt that at the end of 1988 we would probably be heading to Atlanta and Georgia State University.

But the Lord had other plans. In the middle of the 1988 season, while pitching in Tulsa, Oklahoma, I threw a pitch that "fell off the table," meaning that it dropped significantly. I had been working on a pressure sinker that Glenn Abbott, our pitching coach, had taught me. I threw that pitch in a bullpen session and Al Jackson, our Minor League Coordinator, asked me if I could do that again. I told him I believed I could and from that point on I had a major league *pitch.*

Shortly after that, we needed a starter in the rotation in Double A, and they asked me if I would be willing to start. I had been a reliever up to that point with a few spot starts and I said that I would. I had nothing to lose and I ended up going 10-6, winning the ERA title, even though in the first week of August I was called up to Triple A. My first outing in triple A was a two-hit shutout, and I proceeded to pitch extremely well the rest of the season. We lost in the finals of the championship game of the International League. Wade Rowden, who would later join UPI on ministry trips, had the game-winning hit.

I became a free agent by the end of that season, and the Baltimore Orioles signed me. In the spring I went to my first major league baseball camp and began the year with the triple A team in Rochester. I got off to a great start there and was 8-2 in the middle of June. When I was preparing to pitch in Omaha against the Omaha Royals, I was called into the manager's office and was asked by my Triple A manager, Greg Diagini, and my pitching coach, Dick Bosman, if I would pitch that night, or board a plane for Baltimore.

On June 18, 1989, I made my major league debut. The first day I was there, I pitched against the Oakland Athletics in relief and threw three shutout innings. I got a major league save in my debut. It was in front of 46,000 fans and the last batter I had to get out was Mark McGwire. The people rose to their feet. I was able to throw a sinker down the middle that he took for a strike. Then I threw a slider on the outside corner and he hit a weak pop-up to center field, and we won the game.

Two days later, when we were playing in Seattle, I was asked to come into a game. We were losing 5-1 in the first inning when I came in, got a double-play ball, got out of the inning, and shut them out for the next four innings. We took an 8-5 lead against Randy Johnson, and I left the game in the fifth inning after giving up a hit to Harold Reynolds, and then a double to Alvin Davis that scored the first run off me. We were able to shut them down and win the game, and I got my first and only major league win against the Mariners. The highlight of the game was picking off Ken Griffey, Jr. at first base.

Two days later I pitched three innings on Sunday and four and a third on Tuesday. I was still stiff after throwing seven innings in three days and really needed another day off. But in the sixth inning the game was close and they sent me. I got the first out, then gave up a hit, and was facing Jack Howell. On an 0-2 pitch that was supposed to be a sinker away, I threw the ball and tore a muscle in my arm. He swung and struck out but I was done for the next two months. I couldn't raise my arm over my head and wondered if my career would end there.

Again the Lord had other plans. I never regained the same effectiveness after that, even though I pitched from 1989 to 1993 with several trips to the major leagues. I stayed with the Orioles through the next season in which I had my best Triple A season. I was bounced up and down three times between Rochester and the major leagues during that season, finishing 11-1 with a 1.95 ERA. At the end of that season I was traded to the Blue Jays, then to the Phillies in 1992, back to the Mets in 1993, the Colorado Rockies at Triple A in 1994, the Detroit Tigers Triple A team in 1995, and I ended my career with the Florida Marlins in 1996. So my career spanned 15 years, I won over 125 games in the minors, one game in the majors, and had what I feel was an exceptional career for not having great talent. I believe it was a great testimony to the Lord's grace.

My involvement with UPI began in 1986 when I went on my first mission trip to South Korea with Harold Reynolds,

Dave Valle, Jose Alvarez, and Tom Roy. I had been asked by Phil Menzie to go on the trip as Glenn Davis was not able to go, and the trip was paid for. God used that trip to open my eyes to the world. From the time we arrived in Korea to experience the sights, the sounds, the tastes and the feel of the culture, all my senses were touched, and I realized that this was what I had been born to do.

Since 1986 I've been on a trip somewhere in the world every year with UPI. Over the past 22 years I have been in 37 different countries. I led my first trip in 1990 to Bangkok and then in 1991 Tom had me lead a trip to Taiwan, realizing that there was a difficult situation there and he wanted to see how I would handle it. He wanted to test my leadership skills. (I found that out afterwards.)

I have been on six different continents and have had the privilege of seeing people from those continents come to know Christ.

At the beginning of 1996 I realized I was at the end of my baseball career. I was 35 years old and had no desire to be a "Crash Davis" in the minor leagues, hanging on to the game. I really wanted to exalt Christ in my life. At the beginning of that season Tom approached Lisa and me and asked us to pray about coming on part time with UPI in the off-season. It would require our moving from Port Huron, Michigan, where we had made our off-season home, leaving family, and moving to Warsaw. Throughout that season we prayed and sought the Lord and really felt God's direction. Our home in Michigan sold quickly, we found a home in Warsaw, and moved in the fall of 1996.

That fall I also retired from playing baseball, and a week later had a call from the New York Mets, offering a coaching position. I had spent half of my career with the Mets and was excited to have the opportunity to go back to work with many of the coaches who had helped me to progress in my career. I coached with the Mets for three seasons, two at the Rookie Ball level, winning a Rookie Ball championship in the Gulf Coast League with fellow Christian Doug Flynn. My third year I was moved up to A ball, but after three years of coaching, Lisa and I were challenged by Tom to come on full time with UPI as an associate in the international division.

That really was where my heart was. God had worked in my heart to the point where I really just wanted to minister. As a coach I realized I had a job to do and felt like I was doing very well. I also had the freedom to disciple the players. The Mets gave me freedom to do Bible studies and to meet with players one-on-one as long as there was no conflict on the field. I was able to do my job while ministering to the players. Lisa loved the game, loved being able to minister in the game, and felt like she was a great part of it. She was fearful that she would lose the aspect of it being *our* ministry if I went into the ministry full time.

There were many adjustments to make. Tom wanted a decision by September 7, and at 11:55 p.m. on September 11, I e-mailed Tom to say we would come on full time. It was the first time in our married life that Lisa and I did not see completely eye-to-eye on a decision. In obedience to the Lord she said she was willing to follow wherever the Lord was leading. So we made that decision to come on full time with UPI. Looking back on that decision, we have no regrets. We really sensed that was the direction the Lord was leading and are grateful that He has taken care of us each step of the way.

Coming on staff at UPI was a gradual process. After my first with UPI in 1986, I began to go on ministry trips each year. And then I was challenged to lead my first trip and that really began to fire me up, understanding what was required in leading these guys and discipling them on the trip. That was very challenging to me. Each field is different and I love to encourage the players who go on these trips to experience the culture with all five senses, allowing it to get deep down into their spirit. I believe God really impacts their lives as He did mine.

I have learned many practical jokes from Tom Roy, including all the times he has salted my water. On a trip to Far East Russia, when I went to the restroom, he created a pocket in my goulash and just poured hot pepper in and covered it up. When I came back I took a huge bite and really couldn't say anything because Lori Durham had made the meal and I didn't want to offend her. But they all got a great laugh out of it and I got heartburn.

On that same trip we were invited to the home of a kid who was a believer but whose parents and sister were not. He wanted us to meet the parents and, hopefully, begin to build some bridges to be able to share the gospel with the family. We went over there and were told they were preparing what the Russians call a delicacy. At this point I can't remember the name but I called it "chilled chicken fat." It had the texture of Jell-O but it looked like chicken fat and I could not get past that thought. We were all sitting there and I was trying to get it down with bread and with water and just could not get it all down. The family left the room for a moment and just before they walked back in the room Tom flipped his onto my plate and complimented them on the meal. There I was sitting with more on my plate. I told them I couldn't eat it because I had eaten too much borscht and I was full. Tom Roy got me again.

We have had the privilege of seeing several of our clinics turn into church plants. In the Dominican Republic there have been a couple of churches planted as a result of our clinics, and we have been able to show the local church how to conduct sports ministry around the world. I have had the privilege of petting a lion and a tiger, eating exotic foods like zebra, kudu, crocodile, squid, and octopus. We have seen some of the most beautiful places on earth and have had the experience of almost dying while scuba diving in Perth, Australia.

In 2000 Tom entrusted the international division to me to continue international sports ministry and disciple players who invest their time in these trips. My vision is to take teams to all corners of the earth in order to share the Gospel.

What a blessing to have the Westons on board.

When God calls a man into ministry, he really calls the entire family. When Jesus talked with His disciples about following Him, He told them to count the cost. There are sacrifices involved including times of separation. In ministry there are also many who come to you with their pain and heartache. A wife who is committed to the ministry is able to offer prayer support, emotional support, and encouragement. She is the one who takes care of the details of running the home when her husband is away. If the kids believe in what the dad is doing they are better able to handle the separations, knowing Dad is helping others come to know Jesus. The support at home makes it possible for the man to do what he does.

Lisa gives the wife's side of the baseball life. She is a great example of teamwork in ministry. Here is her story:

> I came to Christ as a little kid, about the age of 6. I grew up in a home of first generation Christians and I just really saw in my parents a love for Jesus. The difference Christ made in their lives was just part of my life from the very beginning. I was always at church and learned from my teachers how God loved me and had a plan for my life. It was a very natural thing to realize that I was sinner and separated from God, and that Jesus, through His death on the cross, had paid the penalty for my sin, and I wanted to be part of that. So I trusted Christ as an elementary student and continued to grow in my relationship with the Lord.
>
> I went to college at Eastern Michigan University, and I had enough sense to know that believers can't stand by themselves, so right from the get-go, I found a Christian group on campus that I could be part of. There happened to

be a Campus Crusade for Christ group on my campus. So, right away I became involved in that and a small group Bible study and attended their weekly meetings.

Those four years of college matured me spiritually in ways I had never experienced and, in some ways, have never experienced since. It was a growing time for me, stretching, and learning to share my faith, and becoming even further rooted and grounded in it. It was at one of those Campus Crusade weekly meetings, that I noticed a real good-looking guy wearing a letter jacket from Eastern. He was the emcee of the weekly meetings. That would be Mickey. We actually met at a party.

Mickey and I married right out of college. The New York Mets had already drafted him, so we started on the adventure of minor league baseball that would take us the next seventeen years.

Tom asked Mickey to come on part time as UPI's International Director. The decision that was the hardest was moving away from my family, but we both really sensed that this was what God had for us. It was sad, and we missed our church, but we definitely felt it was of the Lord. Mickey was still playing that summer, but we put our house in Michigan on the market, and I came to Indiana to look for a house. I looked at a couple of houses, but really didn't find anything. When I went back home and pulled in my mom's driveway to pick up my kids, I walked in the door and my mom said, "You have a full-price offer on your house." So, what we had thought to be probably a six- to eight-month process of thinking about moving to Warsaw turned out to be 24 hours, and it was just the Lord saying, "You know what? It's time to go."

I think it might have been just a little bit harder for Mickey, trying to do two jobs at once. He did that for three years in which he coached and then he worked for UPI, in the off-season. After three years, Tom and the board came to Mickey and said, "We really need for you to be full-time." It wasn't a tough decision for Mickey, but it was for me. I loved baseball life, and I loved being part of Mickey's ministry, which was coaching and being part of the players' lives.

Being in coaching was a whole different thing from being a player's wife. We were able to influence guys in a new and different way, and I just watched—Mickey was a great coach. I watched how he influenced guys, how he was able to minister to them, and some for a whole summer. The last summer we coached, we were pretty much at opposite ends of the spectrum as far as should we go on staff with UPI or not. And in the end, to be perfectly honest, I just had to submit because I probably would have said, "I'd rather not." But Mickey felt pretty strongly about it, and I felt like I was his helpmate, and I would do whatever God called him to do.

I could choose to be content, or I could choose to be miserable, and I chose to be content. Our decision to go full-time was good in the end, once I got through that first summer. And, of course, it was the right decision, and Mickey has never regretted it for one minute. It was a perfect-fit job for him.

One of the blessings, I think, of being in the ministry, and being involved with UPI has been watching Mickey come home from a trip so inspired by what happened on the trip. We get to see God's faithfulness firsthand. I think we have seen just how God is so faithful to the ministry of UPI, working out issues that happen on trips and flights, and all kinds of stuff, just seeing how God has been so faithful. It has been a blessing to our family to be in on all that, to hear and see what God is doing around the world. I especially love that our kids have been able to travel with Mickey. Those have been really life-changing experiences for our children, to see the bigger picture of the world, and to see Dad at work, to see what he does in sharing Christ with people. So that has pretty much "flavored" our family, and I love that. It's been great.

Successes are seeing how Mickey's trips pull together even when sometimes it seems like it is not going to happen. Flights change, and we meet up with some more, and it all works out. I love that. And, also, Mickey coming home and talking about not how it changed lives there, but how a trip influences players and changes their lives and the commitments they make when they are on a trip. All of those things, and we hear how encouraged missionaries are from the open doors that it brings to them. Those are the real success stories to me.

I think the heartaches have been more about our family's being separated from Mickey, and I won't say that has been easy. But I guess it's something we have always dealt with even as a player. It's harder on the kids, than it is on me probably, as they see Daddy leave again and ask, "Why does Daddy always have to go?" Now that our children are older, they still question that. "Why does Dad have to go again? Why is he always the one that has to go?" When the kids were little, they needed him in specific ways, and now that they are older, they need him in different ways. So the heartache of it to me is that Mickey misses the milestones in their lives when he's gone. We do a lot to help that and try to stay in touch via e-mail. But I would say that has been the heartache of ministry for our family.

Another blessing of the ministry to me personally, and probably to our family, has been the times we have been able to accompany Mickey to spring training. We generally have had a large house that my folks have helped us get. We enjoy entertaining and having Bible studies and having lots of folks in our house for that month. Mickey does a lot of traveling, but there have been times when he's traveling in Florida, that we have gone with him, and I've gotten to be with other families and wives. I love the aspect of being able to have folks in during spring training, when they're away from their families, to cook for them, and to enjoy Bible studies. That's been a true blessing to me and also our kids, I've heard them relate stories to other friends of theirs, the stories of guys' testimonies that have been shared at a Bible study, or when we've had the baptism of a player. To do special things like that has been a real blessing to me as part of UPI.

I would be remiss if I didn't add something about the wonderful two weeks we spend every summer at Camp of the Woods, (COTW) in Speculator, New York. Tom was the first staff member to go to COTW, followed by Don Gordon. It has been a wonderful blessing to our family to enjoy two weeks at a beautiful camping resort. We have made lots of life-long friends, heard great speakers, have been challenged spiritually, and have gotten to minister ourselves. Mickey, besides doing the baseball clinics every morning, especially these last few years, has done lots of speaking, and it has been so exciting to see kids trust Christ every year at Camp of the Woods. It has been a great privilege to represent UPI at COTW.

In 2008, the Westons moved nearer Chicago to be closer to the White Sox, as Mickey is now their chaplain. Lisa goes on to say,

In the transition we have made from Warsaw to Valparaiso, I am again seeing that as we trust in the Lord, He will faithfully supply all that we need. We had sensed for a couple of years that the Lord was moving us closer to Chicago to be more involved with the White Sox on a regular basis. It has been exciting to see how the Lord has orchestrated the team and the players that are there and the ministry opportunities that Mickey has had especially in 2008 when we moved. It has been hard for our children especially to leave their home in Warsaw, where we had been for twelve years. But I still see God's hand in placing us in Warsaw. What a wonderful place that was to raise children in a very Christian community at a godly, wonderful, caring church that really understood us as missionaries and cared for us (especially me) while Mickey was gone. They were really our family since we were away from family. And that part has been really sad and hard to leave, especially for our children, but again we saw God's hand in selling our home in a really tough market, and then buying a beautiful home in just the right area. I really feel this is what God had for us, and we are seeing that happen and unfold right before our eyes.

I think as our kids look back in a few years, they will also be able to see God's direction. We are experiencing God's provisions for us. The ministry opportunities that Mickey has have been wonderful to see. So again, when we trust God, He is faithful. I don't know why that surprises me, but I love seeing God's hand work in our lives. Getting to be part of UPI has been such a great front row seat to watching God's direction work, not in just our family's lives, but in the ministry and in UPI for His kingdom.

It's Great to be alive because God is in control!

Mickey and Lisa Weston

Action Points

- As the International Director of UPI, Mickey Weston has led many mission trips and has a heart for the world. Have you ever considered being part of a short-term mission trip? Would you be willing to go if an opportunity opened up? Why not tell God you are available if He should ask you to go?

- There are needs all around us. How could you help meet some of those needs? Ask God to bring someone to mind today that needs a kind word or act.

(top) UPI team in Australia: Tom Roy, Roger Mason, Dale Plummer, Mickey Weston, missionary Noel Mitaka

(bottom left) Can you pick out the non-pro baseball player?

(bottom right) Steve Sparks in Thailand

(top) Andy McGaffigan teaches in Hong Kong.

(bottom) Girls come to UPI clinics, too. With Bill Curtis and Mike Steele in Bangkok

(top) Simon Guehring and Chris Singleton speak at a church in Germany.
(bottom) Tony Graffanino and Brian Hommel with players in Mexico

Wearing a Camo Uniform

Playing in the major leagues is the dream of many young men. Bryan Hickerson was able to live that dream. As a pitcher, Bryan was a starter, but in his call up with UPI he began as a reliever.

The ministry in the Phoenix area had grown. Arizona is a hub for spring training and instructional baseball. Many players live there in the off-season as well, and it is a strategic place for developing relationships with players and equipping them. UPI was holding Bible studies and retreats for players as well as providing a chaplain for the new Arizona Diamondbacks.

Bryan, or Hick as we know him, had pitched for the San Francisco Giants, Chicago Cubs, and Colorado Rockies. He also coached two years for the San Francisco Giants organization. Hick had a ministry heart and a no-nonsense approach to life and to God's Word. His heart pumped for truth. He and his wife Jo attended UPI Bible studies, and in 1997 he was invited to join the UPI staff. He began part time and by 1999 he was full time.

Hick became part of the UPI family to assist with the work in Arizona, but after a few years of ministering to players in the Phoenix area, he moved to Warsaw, Indiana, to continue to reach out to players and develop the ministry to U.S. servicemen. He served as co-chaplain for the Chicago White Sox and has led a number of UPI international trips. As of this writing, Hick handles two positions. As the director of the military division, he is in charge of outreach to military bases worldwide. At the invitation of military commanders or chaplains, he sets up trips for pro players to visit troops with the purpose of encouraging them and sharing Christ with them. In addition to that, Hick has taken on much of the administrative work in the UPI office.

Here is what Bryan has to share about his life:

I grew up with a normal, awesome childhood in a midwestern town, loving the outdoors and playing sports. I was never a fan of sports—I just liked to play. I loved playing basketball and baseball mostly and some football in those years. I can't really think of any highlights about that time besides the fun of playing summer and school baseball. I grew up in a Lutheran church and received some good basic Bible knowledge. It was an Awana program at church that challenged me personally as to what it meant to really know God and what it meant to receive Christ. I did that at the age of eleven at a youth camp. Then it wasn't until my first full season, after I had reconstructive elbow surgery in the minor leagues, that another player on the team, who was a believer challenged me to really walk with Christ and to pursue Him as a follower. Not just to receive Him, but to walk in Him. That is where it really started as far as being a disciple and learning more.

In my college years (University of Minnesota) the highlight was being part of a team at that level. Money was not yet involved. Another highlight was that I met my wife, Jo. She ran track at the University of Minnesota. I played for an outstanding group of coaches who cared more about us as people rather than about cranking out high-round draft picks.

I was drafted in my junior year of college by the St. Louis Cardinals but declined to sign. In fact, I wasn't treated that well by the scouts, and they didn't offer me enough money. To me, passing up my senior year and being a part of a team was not worth the $40,000. Eventually I was drafted by the Minnesota Twins and signed with them. I was traded to the Giants my first spring training and spent eight years with them, including four years in the big leagues, then a half season with the Chicago Cubs and a half season with the Colorado Rockies.

I voluntarily retired after being in spring training with the Cincinnati Reds after the 1995 season. I didn't feel I had the passion and drive to maintain the physical and mental level of competitiveness required to stay in the big leagues. I really felt God was calling me to do something else. It was a tough decision, but I believe it was the right one. I really didn't have a plan as to what I was going to do next, but I felt it wasn't to be a player anymore. It was a little scary for Jo and me just to step out and say we weren't going to do this anymore. So I ended up coaching two years with the Giants and then came on staff with UPI.

When I retired from baseball, I thought I would love to be a part of UPI. When I first met the UPI guys, Donnie Gordon and Tim Cash, they met me on the road, and we did studies together. I thought it was great for those guys to be back into that and to be totally sold out and serving God that way, but it's not me. Well, after a few years, God started stirring my heart. So when I got out of the game, I thought that was something I might do, especially after being a part of the Bible studies in the off-season in Arizona. But it wasn't until I went to Ireland with UPI, and a couple of months after that to Bangkok, that I was really impacted about "Serving Christ Through Baseball." It really impacted me then and that was what I felt I wanted to do.

Well, it didn't happen for a couple of years. In fact the same day that the University of Minnesota head baseball coach Don Anderson called my San Jose office (I was the pitching coach with the San Francisco Giants), and said, "Hey, the pitching coach job has opened up, and the job is yours if you want it," Tom Roy flew out to San Jose to meet with me to talk about a position with UPI. I had to make a decision about which way I was going to go. Both were good, but it took months of wrestling with God to figure out where the true passion of my heart was. To invest it in teaching kids at the University of Minnesota to play baseball would have been a totally awesome ministry. But I didn't really have a desire to do it, to put excellence in teaching baseball. I would rather put excellence into the ministry of UPI.

Bryan has become a vital part of UPI. He is very disciplined, committed and intentional. He enjoys the outdoors and staying fit and active. His gifts, interests, and talents make him God's man to lead the military division.

●

We live in a world where global terrorism and extremist ideologies threaten our safety and our freedom. As we look to the future, we believe the coming decades are likely to be ones of persistent conflict—protracted confrontation among state, non-state, and individual actors who use violence to achieve their political and ideological ends. In this era of persistent conflict, the Army will continue to have a central role in implementing our national security strategy. (From www.army.mil)

In 1997 a military chaplain was surfing the net and came across the UPI Web site. He was curious about UPI, so he dropped me a note and asked about the work. Within the week the chaplain began working to have a UPI team visit his base. That was the beginning of the military division of UPI, the ministry of taking professional athletes to visit military bases around the world.

Bryan and Jo Hickerson

The life of a soldier is unique. The military requires discipline and teamwork, and a soldier goes through rigorous training to prepare for battle. Each man has a specific job to do, and he learns how to lead and follow commands. A soldier takes pride in his uniform and strives for excellence. In all of those ways soldiers and professional athletes identify with and have great respect for each other. The obvious difference is that although the athlete risks injury, the soldier risks his life.

That common respect gives the ballplayers an audience and credibility with the soldiers. UPI has been privileged to partner with military chaplains to bring athletes and soldiers together to encourage the troops and for the athletes to share their faith. There is a natural rapport between the soldiers and the athletes. The soldiers look up to the athletes, and the athletes are grateful for opportunities to express their appreciation for the sacrifice of the soldiers.

As the director of the military division, Bryan Hickerson has taken major league baseball players to military bases throughout the world, including war zones like Afghanistan and Iraq. They have had the opportunity to conduct baseball clinics for the children of military personnel and speak at prayer breakfasts, luncheons, and chapel services. They have joined the soldiers in their fitness and readiness drills and have provided counseling for soldiers struggling with life issues. The players have visited wounded soldiers and offered the hope of the message of Jesus Christ.

Many soldiers' lives have been changed as a result of that initial e-mail from a chaplain wanting to help his soldiers.

Kosovo

The first trip by UPI into a war zone was to Kosovo. Much had been in the news about how that country had been ravished by war, and we were excited to have the opportunity to bring Jesus to the soldiers. I had the honor of taking former major leaguers Mike Moore, Sid Bream, and Scott Sanderson. After a short stay in Germany, we flew into Macedonia and drove across the border to Ft. Bondsteel. We had a military escort, and as we drove we saw bombed-out buildings and mass gravesites. It was sobering.

Mike Moore and Scott Sanderson with a soldier in Kosovo

When we finally arrived at Ft. Bondsteel we were graciously greeted and taken to our housing. Camp Bondsteel is quite large— 955 acres located on farmland near the city of Ferizaj/Urosevac. In each direction facing out of the fort, the army had placed tanks with live ammo. We knew from the start we were not in Kansas. This was early in the occupation of Kosovo and the housing was in tents and SEA (Southeast Asia) huts, with five living areas that house up to six soldiers each. We slept in SEA huts with army issue bunks. It was a bed, and we were thankful to be sleeping indoors. The mess hall was in a tent, and the public shower was in another location. (UPI was able to return to Kosovo two more times, and I learned that the facility had improved quite a bit by then—they even had a movie theatre.)

Those soldiers were outstanding men and women. Our ministry included speaking in tented chapels to soldiers who could get away for a Sunday service. There are two chapels on Bondsteel, and Sid and I spoke at both of them. Scott and Mike left the fort that Sunday and were taken in a Humvee to visit soldiers at Camp Monteith. It was a rough, dusty journey that day and as they traveled through the countryside, they were able to see firsthand how the locals lived. Back at Fort Bondsteel I challenged Sid to share a message at the Sunday service. I believe he would tell you today that that experience stretched him. Those men and women were overworked and longing for a word from God, and Sid did a wonderful job of giving them Jesus.

During the week the four of us spent time with commanders and soldiers on location in an attempt to encourage them. One day we helped soldiers put up roof trusses for buildings that were eventually going to replace the tents. It was fun to see soldiers slowly realize that these men were there to work and to serve, and it led to some good discussion. We also had the opportunity to help put in a landing pad for helicopters. I don't know how much work we accomplished, but we were allowed to drive the heavy equipment, and we felt like kids in a candy store.

One of my enduring memories of that trip was how the players ragged on me about my obsession with the Green Bay Packers. We stayed in the chaplain's SEA hut, and he had a computer in his room with wireless Internet. At 3:30 a.m. when I knew the Packers were playing I quietly turned on his laptop and found a site that listed all the plays as they happened. I sat for two hours watching the screen as the other three slept. The Packers scored on the last play to win the game, and I wanted to yell. But I had to wait several minutes until "O dark thirty," the soldiers' 5:30 a.m. wake up call, before I could let it out. Then I went wild. It was another special moment delivered to Packer fans by Mr. Brett Favre.

Others who have been part of military trips since then have had some unforgettable experiences. The following are a few of the accounts of those trips written by both athletes and servicemen:

Afghanistan

"For who is our hope or joy or crown of exultation? Is it not even you, in the presence of our Lord Jesus at His coming?" (1 Thessalonians 2:19, NIV)

How do I begin to describe the experience of this trip? Amazing? Humbling? Exhilarating? Agonizing? An extreme privilege? Yes, all of these…and much more. This page is but a glimpse, a blink of the eye.

Anthony Telford and I (Bryan Hickerson) departed November 20 and arrived home December 9, 2007. During those days we visited six military bases (five in Afghanistan). Besides speaking at chapel services and prayer breakfasts, we visited with as many soldiers as we could, wherever we were. We were invited to go "outside the wire" on a small convoy to bring hot food to a handful of soldiers manning a 155 howitzer. They flew us in a Blackhawk helicopter to visit troops in some of the more remote FOBs (Forward Operating Bases). We were told no one comes to visit soldiers in these places. It was humbling, yet joyful, to see how surprised and thankful they were that someone came.

We were visiting one of the field hospitals as they brought in 18 Afghans who were the victims of a suicide bomber. It was gruesome, but the medics, our soldiers, didn't flinch as they worked to save lives. We had tea with an Afghanistan general and, through an interpreter, learned of their appreciation for our military and the growing hope the Afghans have for their country because of what we've done. The toughest experience was attending a "fallen comrade" ceremony where we stood with countless others, lining both sides of the main road through Bagram to salute one of our soldiers, in a flag-draped coffin, being escorted home.

What was ministry like? Anthony and I continually noted how we felt compelled simply to love and express genuine gratitude for them—and to pray for them. In all of this did we share the gospel? Yes, many times. But not artificially, like an item that needs to be checked off. We're confident the Lord was working in and through us, and during the trip back we often looked at each other and asked, "What is the Lord going to show us about this, in that day when perhaps all will be revealed?" We

both agreed it's something to eagerly anticipate.
Bryan Hickerson, UPI

Anthony Telford and Bryan Hickerson in Afghanistan

Bryan Hickerson, Anthony Telford, and Keith Elias in Iraq

A Soldier's Perspective:

Dear Chaplain Reynolds,

I just wanted to write you a note of thanks for working to bring those professional baseball players to Afghanistan. Let me start by saying I was able to meet Bryan Hickerson back at Fort Drum, and he personally worked with my children at the baseball diamond, teaching them some fundamental baseball skills. This was really nice and meant a lot to my children as well as me. Then what was incredibly encouraging was to see both Bryan and another pitcher buddy of his, Anthony Telford, right here in Afghanistan. I could hardly believe that someone would volunteer their personal time, make tremendous effort, and pay the expense to visit us soldiers here on the backside of the desert. All of that and they don't even get to carry a weapon to defend themselves.

If I recall correctly the whole point of their coming was just to bring some encouragement and love to us soldiers, who at that time were convoying between Bagram and Jalalabad. So when we met them in Jalalabad that night just before we rolled out and they offered to spend some time, sharing a handshake, smiles, and some good old American baseball with us, it was great. They even took the time to pray a blessing over us for our travels. Who would refuse prayer anytime before you go out of the wire? It was an amazing time and was a great delight for my friends and me that night. I hope to see them again maybe back in America, but the fact that they would share their lives with us and then follow up with us here in Afghanistan in the most challenging of circumstances was what made such an impact on us.

Well, again I just wanted to let you know what their time here meant to my friends and me. I know that this really doesn't cover it, but thanks from the bottom of my heart. If you get to talk to them again, let them know that they made an impact on us and we really did appreciate their time and effort.

SPC (p) Richard T. McCutcheon

Another Soldier Writes:

Bryan,

So sorry I haven't responded before now.

As a soldier for 22 years, having the privilege to lead these great men and women of our Army, I identified one area that motivated these soldiers during the hardships of multiple deployments: when visitors or VIPs from our great nation sacrifice their own time and safety to see these troops at their current hostile location.

One unique skill about a soldier that many don't realize is the skill of separating the visitors who truly care and understand what our soldiers are facing today and the burdens that come with it versus the visitors who do not truly understand the burdens the soldiers are facing. The ones that understand and capture the hearts of these men and women are the ones that do not want the special treatment that comes with being the VIP but rather have boots on ground and see and live first-hand what these soldiers face each day.

The visit from Bryan and Anthony was unique and different from many I have seen. Although the soldiers appreciate anyone who visits, there was something special about these two men that captured the hearts of everyone they spoke to. It was not hard as a leader to figure out what separated these men from the visitors we had during this last deployment. They were real, and they were genuine.

Bryan and Anthony, from the first moment arriving, made it known they did not want any special treatment, but rather [wanted to] see and feel what those soldiers actually face. These two men went out of their way to speak and visit with the soldiers and did so in any type of environment or location. Many times soldiers will take the time and, out of respect, show a sense of interest when a visitor speaks with them, but when the conversation is over, they quickly forget the conversation and move on with their duties. When Bryan and Anthony spoke to troops, not only did the troops show a sense of interest, they did not want the conversation to end. On countless occasions the troops approached me just to tell me how much they enjoyed the presence and company of Bryan and Anthony, and more importantly they asked if they were coming back.

Bryan and Anthony truly touched the hearts of our sons and daughters defending this great nation. They did so by being real, genuine, and understanding of the burdens these soldiers face each day. These soldiers and I accepted many "Thank-Yous" from Bryan and Anthony for allowing them to visit, but in reality, we should be thanking them. We defend our country and deploy to these hostile locations be-cause we signed the dotted line to do so, and because of that we are sometimes referred to as heroes. Bryan and Anthony had a choice to visit or not to visit this hostile location. They chose to risk their lives so they could thank soldiers for their service and attempt to touch their hearts, and that they did. These men are the real heroes in our eyes.

Brian K. Knotts, CSM, USA

From a Chaplain:

Bryan,

I believe God used you more than you realize. I don't know if you realize what a testimony it was to those guys that you were willing to put your life on the line to be out where they are. They know that the pagan celebrities from MWR (the group that schedules entertainment for the troops) don't do that, and that in itself is a powerful testimony. Word has traveled all over Regional Command East about the Christian ballplayers who are willing to go out to the remote FOBs (Forward Operating Posts).

The fact that you were even willing to go into the KOP (Korengal Outpost) was an awesome witness. Do you remember the responses you got when you told people that you were going to the KOP? Also you will be able to personally relate to chaplains in a way you could not before. Now you will know what John 10:11 really means.

Chaplain (MAJ) Charlie Reynolds, TF Spartan Chaplain

UPI has also had the privilege to include NFL players on military trips. Here is a letter from one of them:

My Trip to Iraq with UPI

It has been a unique pleasure in my life to have had the opportunity to work with the UPI ministry both at home and abroad. After having worked with Bryan Hickerson, Tom Roy, and Anthony Telford on various trips, including Ft. Bragg and Camp Mackall, to Mountain Home Air Force base and Ft. Wainwright, Alaska, I had an opportunity to travel with Bryan and Anthony to Kuwait and Iraq to speak with our troops downrange in harm's way.

All of us have been given different talents, gifts, and abilities, and all of us who call ourselves Christians must accept that it is our sacred and blessed mission to live out the command of Matthew 28, to go to make disciples of all nations. UPI accomplishes the latter mission by using the gifts, talents, and abilities, namely the experience and prowess of professional baseball players, to spread the truth that there is a God in the universe who loves us desperately and His name is Jesus. UPI uses the platform that baseball has given it to administer the gospel all over the world, and it is in this capacity that I have found true like-mindedness and true friendship among them. As a professional athlete myself (an NFL football player) I ignore the fact that these mere baseball players claim athlete status, and I condescend to join them on their various mission. I am all the more blessed for it.

On our way to Iraq via Kuwait, I was once again thrust together with Hick and Telly, both MLB pitchers, who incidentally are both much bigger than I am, a fact I always have to explain to my defense. What I love about these guys and UPI as a whole is that they get it; they get the fact that all we did was play with a ball, and no matter where we go we know that we aren't there to get our egos rubbed or relive glory days. We are there to serve, to speak words of comfort and encouragement as ministers of the gospel of Jesus Christ, and with that comes a certain responsibility to administer wisdom in our delivery.

Flying out on military transport as guests of Major General Oates and the rest of the command of the 10th Mountain Division, we didn't go over to Iraq with our gospel guns blazing. One of the best things about Hick and Telly is that they understand that sometimes a relationship has to be cultivated before the gospel is harvested. In an environment where young men and women are giving it their all, possibly even their lives, no matter who you are or what you did, if you haven't served, you aren't truly one of them. Understanding this, we knew that it was our job to listen, to hear their stories and their hearts, and then tell them about our Jesus. Consider that if someone is dead asleep in the middle of the night and you barge into their room, dashing on the lights in the process, no matter what you are saying, they will not hear because they'll be too busy burying their faces in their pillows to avoid the light because sometimes light hurts when you're not ready for it. So, it was our task to head out there, be sensitive to the Holy Spirit, build relationships, spend time with soldiers, listening to their hearts, and speaking life into fertile soil. We started doing so on the plane.

We decided before we got there that there would be no task too great or small, that we would be available for anyone at anytime, and we'd sleep when we got home. Right away we were put to the test. After a couple of days in Kuwait, where we immediately struck up conversations with some sailors during lunch, we shipped over to Iraq. We stayed up late, striking up conversations with joes over coffee and got up early (4:30 a.m. early) to do PT (physical training). After devotions together across a man-made lake from Saddam Hussein's Al Faw Palace, we'd set out for the day with Chaplain Charles, speaking to troops, signing autographs, and thanking and encouraging troops—always with an ear cocked to the Holy Spirit, being led in and out of conversations, looking for a chance to take private conversations into the spiritual realm.

During our travels we were treated to a history lesson of the region and an inside scoop of what was going on with our troops in the field. On one hand, I have never been more proud to be an American; on the other it seems our forces have been exploited to a certain degree. Our armed forces are tired—tired from a mission that stretched them beyond capacity. Yes, they have changed the world. Flying over a school on our way to a firebase we witnessed school children come out and wave, their faces bearing the smiles of a thankful people. However, the cost has been high, not in terms of lives lost, though any life is a great cost, but rather in the families that have succumbed to the pressure of moms or dads gone for 15 months or more on various deployments. The cost has included divorces and suicides, and this was articulated perfectly one night as we sat with an officer whom I shall refrain from identifying. After spending some time together where our hearts were mutually discerned, this soldier opened up with barely controlled tears, telling us of the spiritual and emotional fallout of having too small a force and too big a mission.

In our capacity as guests we were afforded a rare opportunity; we were able to speak candidly with privates who drove tanks and answered orders, as well as captains, majors, colonels, and, of course, many starred generals, so we were able to get a picture of this reality from many different points of view. One thing emerged, from generals to sergeants to privates; everyone had sacrificed and everyone hurt in some way and some fashion. Everything came back to God because no matter who you were, there were questions whose answers you didn't have. At one lunch, led by the Spirit, I got to speak with a soldier who told me the bitter story of his divorce and how all he wanted in the world was to get back to his daughter. We prayed together that lunch, and I felt his burden lifted by the One who carries burdens for us all.

That night we spoke candidly with a high ranking officer who told us, "We've become really good at destroying things but not so good at putting them back together." He shared his frustrations in trying to stretch our army into being adept at things they've never trained for. At the same time he is a man who misses his wife, accompanied by a man whose son is in the army as well and he worries for him. Both men carry the pain and hopes of all their soldiers every night when they go to bed and every morning when they rise. Who can comfort them other than the great Comforter? Everything in our trip continually came back to Jesus. And then there was Logan.

Ultimately every trip like this is about people, and we met a rare man indeed. I got to see amazing things in Iraq, places where we dropped missiles and bombs, a Christian chapel on Saddam's compound, Saddam's throne, and many other sights that can fill a historian or archeologist's fancy, but nothing compared to meeting Logan. The entire way out there I felt God preparing me to meet and talk with a Muslim, so I had prepared myself for some unthinkable situations. Little did I know the Muslim would be an Iraqi interpreter, well make that a Kurdish interpreter who spoke Arabic, English, Kurdish, and another language I can't recall. We met in the most fertile ground for sharing thoughts and beliefs—no not the army chapel but the Green Beans Coffee House, where half the camp files through on any given night. If you want to share the gospel, go where the people go. On a night where General Smith accompanied us, much to the astonishment of many soldiers who filtered through there, I struck up a conversation with an unassuming-looking young man because his genuine smile drew me in.

After a bit of small talk, Logan shared his story. At the age of 16 Logan began work as an interpreter for our Armed Forces. Soon, because of his nerve and prowess, he was snatched up by our Special Forces units to do missions with them. We spent most of the night speaking about those very missions. He shared with an electric smile the thrilling details of his life, how he was trained and used. Then his face changed as he recounted the number of friends he has watched die in front of him and in one instance, in his arms. Talk became serious as tears pressed his eyes. We began to speak of life after death, and he shared with me that he is a Muslim. Soon, however, it became apparent that his faith was not giving him any peace. Also, I noticed that he "eyed" up every girl that walked in so I offered, "I thought you were a Muslim?" Logan smiled and answered, "Well, I like the girls. I like the liquor." We both laughed, and I asked him to consider if what he believed was not the truth. We talked a bit, but he stuck firm that he was a Muslim.

The next night as we separated and began opening up conversations with a bunch of different soldiers, there was Logan, talking to a young woman soldier. He saw me and immediately smiled guiltily like a child caught with his hand in the proverbial cookie jar. Soon, we sat down for an earnest chat. I shared my testimony with Logan, and it seemed to have an impact on him. As our second night wore down, his attitude changed from one of disinterest to one of sincere questioning. I gave him a Bible, and he promised he would read and think about the Gospel of John. We said we would meet for lunch the next day, and he actually showed up.

By now I knew God was doing something in this young man's heart, and I began to think of what God could do with a 22-year-old living legend who spoke four languages in a region devoid of the gospel. With the seeds planted, our friendship forged and we left Iraq with a promise. I would always pray for Logan and that he would seek the true God.

We still had a mission to accomplish and it included doing chapel services. I was a bit disappointed by the turnout, but as the chaplains explained, the soldiers get only one day to sleep in, and they take it. There is such a need here for the gospel, but the situation and lifestyle are perfectly set up against it. We had an opportunity to go places and open up conversations the chaplains didn't have, and we used them.

As with all UPI trips, the God encounters come at the most unusual times and nothing goes as scripted. We got stuck in Kuwait on our way home, and it looked pretty bleak. Someone forgot to book us a flight so we were stuck standby, which seemed like it could literally take weeks. Then, God stepped in. Of course we looked at this as an opportunity to show the soldiers and civilians working with us how men of God respond to adversity. Plus, we knew God had something up His sleeve.

The sergeant in charge of us went on a smoke break and ran into a member of the 101st Airborne on his way back to Kentucky. They welcomed us aboard. Not just us, but we had the opportunity to fly home with a special operator as well. Spending the night together, waiting for the flight was the perfect opportunity to minister to these soldiers in a celebratory but somewhat strenuous situation. They were going home for the first time in 15 months, and many had no idea what they were really returning to. I had the good fortune to ride home next to a West Point grad major who just kept telling me how he couldn't wait to sleep. These men were tired. That night I got to share my story many times over, and watched as each soldier processed it in a different way. I made friends with the special operator who shared his faith with me, and we were able to be mutually encouraged.

We will never know, this side of eternity, the impact that these trips had on the soldiers we spoke to and shared with. Well, except in one special case. It was December 23 when my cell phone rang. Answering it, I was pleasantly surprised when the voice on the other end was Logan's. I immediately asked how he was able to call, and he said he was on a mission and took a satellite phone from a special operator. I asked him if the FBI was about to kick in my door. He laughed. He wished me a Merry Christmas and then told me something I will never forget. He told me he read the Bible I gave him, he read the Gospel of John, and he learned something. He learned that Jesus is not the Son of God, but he is THE God. I immediately asked Logan if Jesus was his God and Logan said, "He's everybody's God." Logan told me how, after reading the gospel he prayed to God so that he could put his faith in Jesus. And that is what it's all about. Mission accomplished.

Hold on to your hat when you take a trip with the men of UPI. You never know where God will bring you, but you know it will have eternal significance, and it will be a blessed ride. I will be forever thankful to be involved, in some small way, with the ministry known as UPI.

Keith Elias, Former NFL Running Back

From Other Military Trips:

Thank you for your service to God and to all of us deployed to Kosovo.... it was a powerful experience, and an oasis in the desert that deployments can sometimes become. Thank you for your example. God is indeed *great* and *good* beyond all measure!"

COL Alan Landry

I can never tell you how profoundly your visit affected me. No one comes up here to Alaska, really. For the soldiers to meet their baseball idols with a positive message and show you in return what we do is just tremendous. I am still as excited as a kid.

CSM Tim Green

The visit from UPI blessed the soldiers of 1-63 Armor Battalion. From visiting in staff offices with Officers and senior NCOs (non-commissioned officers) to crawling on an Abrams tank in the rain, the players' genuine concern for people came through. Soldiers appreciated their visit; one citing their great thanks for someone caring enough to come out to a range, in the rain, to visit them and show appreciation for the American soldier. The players gave clear witness to the life-changing power of Christ in one-on-one encounters and group discussions. UPI has the unique gift of bringing the gospel through their doorway of sports.

Chaplain (Captain) Ken Godfrey

It takes a special kind of person to serve in our military. I'm grateful for their willingness to protect our country. Whenever I've gone to spend time encouraging them, I'm the one who walks away from it being blessed. I'm honored to be used by God in this way.

Scott Sanderson, UPI board member and former MLB player.

It is an honor to be able to encourage and share our faith with men and women in our military. Through baseball God has taken us so many places we would have never gone. Who would have thought that baseball would be the reason we were blessed to go and share the gospel of Jesus Christ to the people who serve and protect our nation? It was an awesome opportunity to go with UPI to a base to share the love of Jesus Christ.

Cal and Christy Eldred, former MLB player, UPI board member and his wife

There are many parallels in the military life and professional athletics. It was a natural fit to speak to the soldiers on some of the victories, adversities, and how my relationship with Jesus has given me solid footing on which to stand throughout my career. I look forward to future opportunities to encourage and support our troops in bases throughout the world.

Shawn Boskie, former MLB player

We serve an awesome God. I knew going to a military base would be a great opportunity to minister and serve, a chance to bless the soldiers. I returned home a very proud American, and I want to say thanks to the men and women who serve our country. God Bless America!

Tim Hulett, former MLB player.

Hunting Division

A number of professional athletes like to wear camo uniforms, too—not for military purposes but for hunting. UPI launched a hunting division unofficially in 1999 when Jed Hansen, former player, followed up a UPI military trip to Ft. Wainwright in Fairbanks, Alaska, with a wild week of hunting with Dave Neetz, Mike Valentine and me. We loaded Dave's van and drove as far as the road would take us to Circle, Alaska. Then our pilot flew us another 170 miles to a remote location and dropped us off. I had never really camped outdoors, much less in the Alaskan wilderness. Dave and Mike were experienced hunters, but Jed and I had never really hunted before. When that plane left us, we knew we were in for an adventure. Jed tells it like this:

> We went on a hunting trip that was incredible—hunting moose. It was awesome! It was like a man's dream adventure just to be out in the middle of wild country—Dave Neetz sleeping with his shotgun in his sleeping bag because of Grizzly bears, and Valentine sleeping with his 44 Magnum, or whatever that hand-held cannon was. Playing chess all day on Sunday because it had snowed the night before and all day on Saturday. There was about a foot of snow and it was like 18° below. It had been 50 degrees the day before and was 53 degrees two days later.
>
> We tracked a moose and I shot *at* it. There I was (I had never shot a rifle except a BB gun when I was little), going hunting for the first time. We tracked the moose into a little clearing. I thought Dave would take a shot, so I crept up a little bit closer. The moose was about a hundred yards away, which is a pretty good distance, but when you are shooting a rifle, I was told, it is like trying to throw a rock into the ocean. Somehow my rock didn't make it into the ocean three times. I shot once when the moose was broadside, and he looked up, turned his whole body toward me, so he was facing me. I shot and missed again, and the moose probably thought,

"Some peon has never shot a rifle before; I'll show him the broad side again." I shot at him again—and missed. Dave Neetz said, "Shoot again." I said I was out; my gun was empty. But we tracked down the moose, and Dave brought his big cannon and in one shot dropped the moose.

I guess the way to describe it would be like playing in the World Series, having never played baseball before, but having dreamed of it. It's like being in the grand arena, facing Roger Clemens, who mistakenly throws you three fastballs right down the middle and you swing and miss—three times. Hunting in Alaska and getting an opportunity to shoot a moose was like that. Everything was incredible, and then I missed. That was kind of a neat experience. Fast-forward to hacking that moose apart with a hatchet. I think you call it "caping." It weighed 1500-1800 pounds and had a 63-inch rack. Dave cut the moose hide off neatly from the shoulders up so he could mount it. That night we ate the heart of the moose, which I guess, is a "rite of passage" type thing. It was an interesting steak, about the size of my head. We cooked it over a fire and ate it that night and we had some of the filet the next night.

That was a really neat, fun experience, and I'd do it again in a heartbeat if I could. Only this time I would take my fly rod and go fishing the whole time.

As much fun as that trip was, I realized the time around the campfire at night was even better. Jed was at least 20 years younger than the rest of us. Here are his thoughts: "I remember sitting around the fire a couple of nights and asking you guys questions about life. Just simple questions like 'What would you do differently in your life?' And the stuff you three shared with me meant a lot on that trip, and it had a very positive influence on me."

The wheels were turning as I thought through how UPI might include hunting as an opportunity to disciple ballplayers. Many doors have opened since that trip, and the hunting division of UPI was launched. Many baseball players enjoy hunting. There is just

(top) Jo Hickerson, Christi Eldred, and Cal Eldred with soldier in Fairbanks, Alaska

(bottom) Bryan Hickerson, Anthony Telford, and Keith Elias with troops at Ft. Bragg

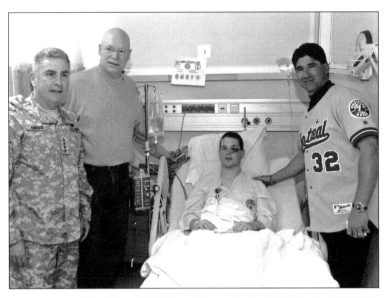

(top) General John Abizaid, Joe Urcavich, and Anthony Telford visit Purple Heart soldier in Germany.

(bottom) Chaplain Dave Neetz with Noah Herron of Green Bay Packers football team

Mike Matheney with deer

something about getting out the "camo" and getting ready for white-tail season. There is enough interest among players that UPI tries to conduct at least one hunt a year. Led by Cal Eldred, UPI sets up hunts to bring baseball players together during the off-season.

The typical whitetail hunt begins at 5 am with a pot of coffee before heading out to the hunt location with weapons and hunting gear. Several hours are spent in the tree stand with time to think. Around eleven the hunters climb down from the stands, hopefully to gut their animals. After a long walk back and a big lunch we settle in for a time in the Word. Usually one of the UPI staff leads this time of informal teaching and discussion. The men talk about what God is doing in their lives. Then it is back to the tree stand for more time to watch and think. This has been a great tool for reaching deeper into the world of baseball--players who love to hunt.

UPI continues to seek ways to reach the world of baseball.

It's Great to be alive because God is in control!

Action Point

- Please pause to pray for our troops. Why not send a note of encouragement to a soldier or the parent of a serviceman?

Bring in the Lefty

At this writing the most recent addition to the UPI family is Brian Hommel. From the first day the staff met Brian we all liked him. He was young, single, funny and full of life. And he loves Jesus.

Here is Brian's story:

I was born October 26, 1972, in Hutchinson, Kansas. My dad worked for the American Restaurant Association (ARA), and we moved a lot. We moved 13 times in my first twelve years, so my sister and I became very transient kids.

We were living in San Antonio, Texas, when my parents decided to go into the restaurant business. We had a small deli downtown, located about a block from the Alamo, and an Italian restaurant named Stromboli's, located on the side of town where we lived, so I grew up around the food business. I went to work with my dad at 4:45 a.m. because we served breakfast and lunch downtown. He and I ran the deli. We had someone take orders, Dad cooked, and I did dishes and odds and ends.

That was a hard time. I loved my mom, dad, and my sister, but it's tough running your own business. It is hard on your family. My family allowed me to play sports, however, which was an avenue that helped me connect with other kids. I transitioned well to new schools because of playing sports. I was able to have a group of friends immediately and fit right in, which was great.

I came to know Jesus at a church camp where my parents sent me when I was eleven. I went with one of my friends and I didn't know it was a church camp until the last day I was there. I was sitting on my bunk next to our counselor, and he asked if anyone wanted to ask Jesus into his heart. If anyone did, he said he would pray with him. To be honest, that was the first time I had ever heard of Jesus. I prayed the prayer, and honestly I felt like I rose right off my bunk. I am not saying that my relationship with Christ is all emotions, but there are emotions involved. Man, I had such an overwhelming feeling. I went home, and my sister, who was then 16, said, "Hey, what's wrong with you?" I said, "There is nothing wrong." There was such a peace in my soul. I can remember it to this day.

Prior to moving to San Antonio when I was 9, we lived in St. Joseph, Missouri, in a church building that was converted into a house. My mom bought a children's Bible and read it to us one time. So when I came back from the summer camp, I asked my mom if she still had that Bible, and she did. I took it to my room and read it when I went to bed every night for the next three years of my life. So that was my church—no corporate worship; we never went to church. I diligently read all the way through that book.

At the end of eighth grade I was working quite a bit at our family restaurant, Stromboli's. It was the beginning of a time in my life when I made some poor choices that brought me much pain and suffering. I look back on that time with a lot of remorse. A 23-year-old married woman with two kids was a cook at the restaurant. I ended up in a hotel room with her, and I remember that afterward I went into the bathroom and wept. I thought God was done with me, that He no longer loved me. I had broken one of His command-ments. I remember curling up in a ball between the toilet and the tub, feeling afraid and alone.

Right after that we moved to Indianapolis where I kept it to myself and buried the pain. However, the pain was still there, so I threw myself into sports, figuring it was a good way to escape the pain. I got involved in baseball and football and had great success in both sports. My senior year I made first All-State in Indiana and was first in wins, in ERA, (earned run average) and second in strikeouts. I was granted a full ride scholarship at the University of Louisville. During my freshman year I started getting involved in partying.

Finding my worth in baseball by getting wins and strikeouts, I was spending time with the guys on the team and having a good time from a worldly standpoint. But I found myself unsatisfied. Trying to satisfy myself caused more pain within my soul. I became involved in gambling, I almost lost my scholarship, and I was suspended 14 games by the NCAA for gambling. I lost a lot of money gambling. I also had been with several different women, just one-night stands because I didn't want to see them again. It was agony for me, and it wasn't bringing joy, just more pain.

April 1993 brought a huge turning point in my life. The gambling, the girls, and the grades were terrible. I tore the ACL in my right knee and was out of baseball for a year, and at that time baseball was everything to me. I couldn't perform and I couldn't fight, so I just drank. I met a girl from England at a bar, and I gave her my number. She called me up and we got together, and when she left I thought she was probably pregnant. I remember calling my sister Tab, and she said, "You have to repent."

That night I did. I cried for what seemed an eternity but was probably just a few hours. Man, I was so sick of my journey, my pain, and my sin. I laid it all out to Jesus. I didn't even think He wanted to hear it, to be perfectly honest, but I had to. As I wept, I fell asleep on the floor—on my knees and on my face. When I woke up the next morning, it was as though Jesus had wrapped His arms around me and had just loved on me, and I was at the top of the steps shouting, "I'm free!" I was free, as I experienced forgiveness.

I was the prodigal son coming back home, and a whole new life began for me. Before, it felt like I wasn't able to please my team, my coaches, or my family because of my failure on the mound. It was painful to feel that I wasn't able to satisfy anybody, including myself. When I was able to release that, it changed me. I finished two more years at the university and was drafted in the 21st round of the major league baseball draft my junior year. At that point I was willing to be used by God in any way He chose.

Shortly after God had revealed Himself to me and I was freed up, I got a letter from the Blood Bank. I remember taking the letter outside on the porch of my apartment and thinking, "AIDS!" based on my promiscuous lifestyle. "Jesus," I prayed, "If I have AIDS, I want you to know that I will serve you with every last breath that is in me because I was headed toward hell and you rescued me and delivered me into the kingdom of heaven. So I will do whatever it takes, and I praise you for every moment I have left in my life." It turned out the letter was asking for a blood donation, but it set the tone for how I wanted to spend my life—with great gratitude and thankfulness.

As Brian mentioned, he attended the University of Louisville on a baseball scholarship. At the end of his junior year in June 1995, he was drafted and signed by the Milwaukee Brewers. He was committed to Jesus at the time, and in his mind's eye he thought he could see God's plan. He would make it to the big leagues and be a witness for Jesus. That had to be God's plan, right? So he left his home in Indianapolis with that in mind. It was not long until his perspective was challenged and changed.

Brian started his pro career in the short season league in Helena, Montana. He had success on the field, appearing in 15 games with an unbelievable 0.45 ERA. He had 32 strikeouts in 20 innings of work out of the bullpen with a 2-0 record. Not a bad start. But off the field his life was a wreck.

In spring training in Arizona in 1996 Don Gordon invited him to attend a UPI Bible study. Many active players and their spouses attended the study. Although Brian loved baseball, he was focused on his own career and didn't know many of the players. At that study Don asked if anyone wanted to share with the group what Jesus was doing in their lives. Brian immediately got up, went up front, and started to share his heart about how he had just come out of a bad relationship and how Jesus was working on him. Typically other guys did not go up front to share, but Brian did not know that—he just did what seemed right to him.

The players loved him. He was so transparent and fresh in his approach to faith and life. He is still that way today. The wives wanted to know more about his dating life. It became part of the humor among them to follow Brian's social life. They all embraced Brian.

In the fall of 1996 Don invited Brian to make a missions trip to Ireland. The team would consist of Bryan Hickerson, Don Gordon, Shawn Boskie, and a policeman named Steve. A few months later Brian found himself on a plane headed toward Dublin. On the flight

Brian Hommel, Damen Thames, and Kyle Abbott in Italy

he listened to a Third Day CD and was overcome with the fact that God would use him. Brian was amazed how much joy it brought him to work with and love on the kids. He loved what UPI did and loved being a representative for Jesus.

The 1996 baseball season was a short one for Brian because of injuries and surgery to repair his knees.

In 1997 Brian took his second UPI trip and headed to the Philippines with Bryan Hickerson. By the end of the year he had also traveled to Germany with me and to South Africa with Lee Tunnel. During the off-season in 1998 Brian and I traveled to Bolivia together. He was developing a strong bond with UPI, and he says he is grateful for the way Don, Tim Cash, and I invested in his life.

Brian played for two more seasons and when his professional baseball career ended in 1999, he made it very clear to us that he wanted to come on staff with UPI. But Brian remembers the dead silence that met his announcement. He was dumbfounded at our lack of enthusiasm. Now he looks back and realizes that he was young, single, and needed some seasoning.

He took a job working with the youth at Second Baptist Church in Houston. He also supplemented his income by doing pitching lessons at Baseball USA. It was in Houston that he met and married Kim Casey. I was highly honored to be asked to perform the wedding ceremony. Finally in February 2001, I called Brian to offer him a position with UPI. He remembers that when he told Kim the news, they both cried. This was what he wanted to do with his life and Kim was on board.

In July the Hommels arrived in Warsaw. They said good-bye to good friends and packed up their belongings to make the long cross-country trip from Phoenix. It was the practice back then for UPI to close the office during the week of the All-Star game, and Brian hit it just right—his first week on the job was a vacation week. The following week he went to Maranatha Bible Conference in Muskegon, Michigan, to conduct baseball clinics. He spent two weeks on the beautiful Lake Michigan shore. He thought, "This has to be the greatest job on the planet!"

Brian said that when he first came on staff, although he enjoyed travel and ministry, his heart was to be part of UPI for his own personal growth. He wanted to know God deeply and believed that being part of the UPI staff could help bring that about. He loved every man on the UPI staff and felt they would help shape and direct his life and move him closer to God. He says that is exactly what happened and is still happening today.

Brian remembers his four months in Warsaw as a time of my pouring into him and challenging him with how *to be with* God rather than how *to do fo*r God. He was given two assignments while in Warsaw. He was to write two papers, one on the Holy Spirit and the other on covenants. I gave him these topics because I knew they could impact him for the long haul in working with players. Brian admitted that he wanted to prove his worth, not just "be." But it was a good time for him to learn about himself and his relationship with God.

After their time in Warsaw, Brian and Kim were asked to move to Atlanta to work with Tim and Barb Cash. As a part of Brian's leadership training, I felt it would be good for him to be with Tim, but also for Tim to have a chance to train the next UPI guy. The Cash family and the Hommels became very close. Brian learned a lot in the 18 months he spent in Atlanta. He feels it was a life-changing time. Tim showed him how he operated, ministered, and guarded his family time. This was all really cool to Brian. Tim allowed Brian to connect with the Atlanta Braves but also emphasized that Brian just needed to *be*.

Brian's time in Atlanta ended abruptly when Don Gordon resigned from UPI. There was a vacancy now in Arizona, and Brian had been trained to move into the fire of leadership and full-time responsibility in the big city. So in September of 2003, they made the move to Phoenix.

It was a tough transition for the Hommels. They arrived in Arizona as the new kids on the block. Brian had spent many hours learning from Tim, but now he had to step up to the plate and lead. He wanted to be an encouragement to players and their families. He already had a heart for developing deep relationships and he had a passion for sharing the gospel. Now he found himself desiring to pour deeply into souls. He desired to see Jesus change lives in significant ways.

In 2004 Vince Nauss of Baseball Chapel asked Brian to become the chaplain for the Arizona Diamondbacks, and Brian accepted. He was still passionate about mission trips, learning different cultures, and ministering to the poor and hurting. But he was also excited about connecting the rich and hurting with Jesus.

The Hommels now have three beautiful daughters, Abby, Ellie, and Selah, and God continues to mold Brian for His kingdom. His duties with UPI include setting up and leading Bible studies for the players who live in the Phoenix metro area during the off-season as well leading three studies a week during spring training each year. He is also involved in setting up outreaches in the U.S. during the season for the purpose of reaching the lost for Christ through baseball. Brian is chaplain for the Arizona Diamondbacks, and in 2008 he published *Dropping the Fig Leaves*. The book deals with authenticity and challenges us to drop our pretenses and be genuine. Brian states, "I have gone through different phases in my life. It has been a joyous time with UPI, and I hope I can end my life with UPI."

It's Great to be alive because God is in control!

The Brian Hommel family

Action Point

- Brian has written *Dropping the Fig Leaves*, dealing with vulnerability and transparency (available at www.upi.org). What are some ways you could become more transparent?

As UPI expanded from clinics and camps to international outreach, it became clear that the Lord was also leading us to go deeper with the athletes. Pros continued to take part in trips and outreaches, but there were many players who were hungry for greater depth in their Christian walk. Each of the staff had developed relationships with players and the need for discipleship was increasing, especially in Arizona and Atlanta. Bible studies were established in Atlanta, Arizona, and in spring training and they were going full force.

Here is how Tim Cash describes the studies in Atlanta:

The History of the Men's Bible Studies in Atlanta

We moved to Atlanta October 11, 1993. It's interesting that when Tom and I talked way back in the beginning that we were about *being* and not to worry about *doing,* we were just to observe to see what God opens up. That is what happened in Atlanta.

I started meeting with Greg McMichael and shortly after that Brett Butler joined in, two guys I knew but not at a real deep level. After a while, Barb got involved in a girls' Bible study with some of the wives, and that is how I met Terry Pendleton. I started bonding with TP, and he prayed to surrender to Christ. He had already prayed a prayer to Christ for salvation and now he started tracking with the men. It was the same with John Smoltz. We met shortly after, and the door swung open into his life. Then we started to meet with some of the Braves and other players that lived in this area. Paul Byrd began coming and I started bonding with Jason Varitek and Chris Reitsma as well. More men followed, including Jeff Foxworthy, Ernie Johnson Jr., John Burrough, Lester Archambeau and Todd Peterson. It was a good start to the journey.

We started to meet in the back room of a barbeque joint called JR's. My buddy, Tim Shaw, who is part owner of JR's, has been "off the charts" gracious to us. JR's has become sort of our church hangout. I tried to create a place where guys could be real. When these guys go to a church they are constantly surrounded and worshiped. I wanted a place where guys could get away and get raw and real–become really stripped down and not put on a pedestal.

I went on a trip with Jeff Foxworthy and his brother Jay. Jay was moving to the north side of Atlanta near where I live, and he said he would really give anything if there was a Bible study close by. So he and I began to pray about a businessmen's study. It came together shortly after our meeting.

Our pro guys' study has been meeting on Thursday mornings for years. We meet from 9:15 to 11:30 am. with guys like Smoltz, Foxworthy, Ernie Johnson, John Burrough, Paul Byrd, Ned Yost—there are so many guys. The businessmen's study meets from 6:30 am to 9:00 am. with guys like Tom Tabor, Bruce Coker and Mark Parker. It has really grown. Smith Peck and his family, Ron Brasfield and Jay Foxworthy have kind of been the "glue" of the group. There are 18 to 20 businessmen who are being trained in the Word and having fellowship. It has become a pretty cool part of UPI.

A New Effort in Phoenix

A second hub for discipleship is Phoenix. Brian Hommel had been trained by Tim and wanted to model what he saw in Atlanta. Here he tells of that transition:

When Kim and I left Atlanta for Arizona in September 2003, we embraced the new journey. We had been under the leadership of Tom in Warsaw, along with Hick and Mickey, where I had spent six months learning how to live life just "being." Then we moved to Atlanta for 18 months where we learned a lot from Tim and Barb Cash. Once again, it was a time of "being" more than "doing." I was being prepared to lead. When we moved to Phoenix I was immediately put into that position. But we were both leaving good friends behind.

The transition was pretty tough. Don Gordon had led the study for eleven years and I had attended those studies under him when I first lived here from 1996 to 1999. Many saw me as a young kid involved in the small group doing studies with them. We were now asking them to look at me as a leader. I had wondered how they would receive me since I was younger than a lot of them who had been involved. There was a good chance they would see me only as a little brother.

I struggled with that. At times I tried to prove myself and do things differently, even radically, but later I realized I didn't need to do it like that. I had to learn that I just needed to be who I was in Christ and be confident in that. I wasn't here to compete, I wasn't here to compare with what took place in the past, I was here to do what God called me to do right now.

It was a little bit of a grind at the beginning. Clearly there was a transition taking place but I felt that God was bringing some cool things into place. I started thinking geographically, wondering where would be the best place for the studies. I did not want to have a study where it had always been just because it had always been there.

I started developing relationships with players in the northern part of Phoenix. I knew it was crucial to find some people who would be the core of the group. I was looking for people who desired genuine growth in Christ and who wanted to grow alongside me.

It's cool to have people who want genuine growth in Christ. In that context there are certain people you connect with who you trust and who are movers. We were able to find those couples early on, and they are the couples who are still involved today, years later, and that has been a real blessing to Kim and me. We now have a number of discipleship Bible studies much like Tim has in Atlanta. We attempt to be very relational as we wrap around the truths of God's Word.

During the off-season, studies are held for the couples one night a week from 5-7 p.m., typically in someone's home. We also do a men's study from 6:30 to 8 a.m. once a week. Another venue is Spring Training. This is a very busy time as we meet from 7-8:30 p.m. at three locations around Phoenix. The spring training sites for the teams determine these locations. Both men and women are invited. It is a great way to gather at the beginning of their season to discuss what is really important in the many long days that make up the pro baseball season.

The book, *The Tale of Three Kings* ministered to me greatly in the beginning of this transition. I needed to trust God that everything was going to be all right. As long as I was seeking His face, it didn't matter whether anybody showed up to a study I was leading. I had to be confident in that, and I still need to remember that today. I can't base the effectiveness of ministry on numbers but on the greatness of the King and His love for me.

One really cool aspect of equipping players here in Arizona has been the annual UPI Men's Retreat. Each January we spend a weekend in the mountains for the purpose of getting away from the hectic schedules and concentrating on the goodness of God. We have been blessed to have many good speakers and 30 to 60 men attend those retreats. Many talk about how life changing those times have been.

Kim has been a great wife and friend. The transition was tough on her, as she had to leave good friends behind. She was forced into new relationships and a lot of the wives were not necessarily willing to embrace her immediately. She has been tremendous in how she has dealt with it. One of the hard parts about living in Phoenix is that the people are transient. People come and go. Kim and I knew we needed a group of people that we could pour into year round. We have established a small group that meets all year. These are not ballplayers but just people who love Jesus and us.

We have been very thankful that UPI put us in a position to stretch us. Arizona has been a real learning experience for which we will be forever grateful.

Additional Avenues for Ministry

Another side of discipleship is the partnership between UPI and Baseball Chapel. Under the leadership of Vince Nauss, Baseball Chapel provides chapels for every professional team during the season. Each of the UPI staff members has had ministry at the Major League level as a result of the partnership with Baseball Chapel. As of this writing Tim Cash is the chaplain for the Atlanta Braves. Brian Hommel is the Arizona Diamondbacks chaplain, and Mickey Weston is chaplain for the Chicago White Sox. Bryan Hickerson served as co-chaplain with Mickey for several years, and prior to that I was the chaplain for the Sox for five years. These positions have given UPI direct contact with current players, managers, coaches, and front office personnel, as we minister in the locker rooms.

Under Vince's fine leadership a system was devised so each major league chaplain is responsible for assigning chaplains and for follow up with each minor league team within their organization. This opens up relationships with many players and others who follow Christ in the minor leagues. It's a great opportunity for ministry afforded UPI by Baseball Chapel.

We have also been blessed to see new ministries birthed as a result of participation with UPI. Some of these included Glenn and Teresa Davis opening Carpenter's Way, a home for abused children, Dave and Vicki Valle starting Esperanza, a ministry to people of the

Dominican Republic, and Lee Tunnel starting a Christian traveling baseball team. Others got involved in ministries with youth and inner city kids. Ted Barrett, a Major League umpire, along with fellow umpire Rob Drake, started Calling for Christ, a retreat ministry to disciple umpires. Here is what Ted has to say:

CFC started with an idea God laid on both Rob's heart and mine at the same time. We wanted to have an umpire retreat but had no idea how or where to begin. We both attended the UPI retreat in Prescott and you sat at our table. It was there that we began to formulate a strategy to form CFC. Later that year I met Dean, a pastor from Oklahoma, and asked him to help. The UPI staff has been a huge help to all of us in this ministry. Brian Hommel came and taught at the initial CFC retreat in 2003 and has been a constant source of godly assistance. I have been blessed to be involved in several UPI outreach events and several UPI retreats and they have been invaluable to my spiritual growth and my growth as a leader in the CFC ministry.

With the discipleship side of UPI thriving, as well as the International Division under Mickey and the Military Division under Hick, I was sensing it was time for change. What direction would God take the ministry in the future? Were there new areas of ministry for UPI to explore?

It's Great to be alive because God is in control!

Former players Pat Combs and Stan Leland with MLB umpire Ted Barrett

Action Point

- Have you ever sensed the Spirit of God nudging you toward doing something new in your life?

- What are your talents and abilities? What is your passion in life? Have you ever wondered how God might use you for the sake of His kingdom?

Transition

If you were born before 1980, you understand how much the world has changed. It is difficult to keep up with the changes in technology alone. Times change and so do ministries, and they need to.

In the early years of UPI we sometimes pulled off the road to find a phone booth to call to a player. Today we have cell phones, text messaging, e-mail, and the Internet with sites like MySpace, Yahoo, and Facebook, instant messaging, digital audio recorders, and Skype along with many other tools of communication. The communication industry has boomed and changed the way we conduct ministry.

Change is inevitable in ministry, and the time comes to pass on the mantle of leadership. I was getting older and the players were getting younger. From the inception of UPI it has been critical to me that the ministry not be about me and that it would continue as long as there were people who needed the message of Christ.

From the time I turned 50, transition has been on my mind, and I sincerely wanted the transition in this ministry to honor the King. I have seen some ugly transitions in the Christian community. Leaders often hang on to their positions long after the ministry has grown beyond their ability and energy. Sometimes new leadership is assumed for the wrong motive, at the wrong time, or in the wrong way. Was it possible to transition in a way that demonstrated the body of Christ working together in unity?

With that in mind, I first opened the transition topic at our board meeting in October 1997. I asked the board what my job should look like down the road and how long I should stay with UPI. Carin was very reluctant for me to ask those questions. She did not want the board to feel I wanted out. I assured her that I had a few years left, but it was a subject that needed to be addressed directly.

The topic surfaced again at a June board meeting in 1999 when I handed out a newsletter from *Focus on the Family* outlining their plan of succession. I challenged each board member to look over that newsletter and come up with ideas for UPI. We needed to discuss this issue so we would be prepared when the time came for me to step aside.

At the next board meeting in October of that year, board chairman Randy Swanson said, "Tom is no longer a spring chicken." The board challenged me to be more selective in my scheduling. The minutes stated, "Tom's role is now primarily the CEO, mentor and visionary with Tim and Don the primary voices for UPI in the various parts of the country." After that meeting I spent less time on the road and more time in the office handling the day-to-day decisions and duties of a director.

The board continued the discussion on succession, stating that there were two ways it could happen: 1) choose a new director from the outside or 2) choose someone from inside. They said succession could happen quickly or gradually over a period of time. A gradual process was favored. At that meeting it was decided that "should something happen to Tom so that he is unable to fulfill his duties as Executive Director, a successor from the UPI staff would be selected by the Board of UPI to serve as Interim Executive Director until such time as the Board appointed a full-time Executive Director." The wheels were in motion.

A few years later Tim became the National Director of UPI with increased responsibilities. He was now to be totally responsible for the activities and communication with the staff during the season from mid February through September. That freed me up to work on other aspects of the ministry for those months as well as to take time away for vacations and refueling. It also allowed me to see how the staff would respond to my not being there, keeping in line with my leadership style. Sure enough, I would hear concerns about my not being there for them during the season. The plan was working. Tim had been with the ministry longer than any other staff members. He has great energy and a great passion for ministry with athletes. He was also a mentor to the staff in many ways. Tim was my obvious replacement if the board were to choose from within.

Again in April of 2005 I asked the board what my position should look like with UPI for the next 10 years. The men on the board felt that Tim and I complemented each other and that Tim seemed to be the natural successor. Later that year I approached Tim with the idea of his becoming the Executive Director, but the time was not right for him. He had concerns about how it might change his ministry with the players.

At that same meeting I asked that Tim be added to the official board to give him an opportunity to have training and input, to get to know the board better, and to understand the work of the board. I also wanted the men on the board to have the opportunity to see Tim's heart. Tim became a non-voting member for one year. In August of 2006 Tim became a full voting member of the board. Now both Tim and I would be reporting on ministry and voting at the board level.

The final step in moving Tim to the position of Executive Director was a strategic planning meeting with Tim, businessmen Brad Gutwein, Brian Shepler, and me. This was the fourth strategic planning session in the history of UPI. These strategic planning sessions have always been a great benefit to the ministry, giving focus to who UPI is and what direction we should take.

The meeting was in Chicago and we spent two-and-a-half days working through the vision and direction of UPI. We had great discussions, and other meetings followed by phone and email. Eventually a plan was delivered to the board, detailing what UPI should look like in the future. Here's that plan.

Unlimited Potential, Inc. Ministry Strategy

Introduction

As UPI nears its 30-year anniversary of ministering to the professional baseball community, several recent developments have positioned the organization for accelerated growth and increased kingdom impact in the coming years.

More than ever, UPI enjoys a unique position and opportunity to significantly impact the 9,000-member professional baseball community. Over the next five years, the primary elements of UPI's strategy will include:

- doubling the number of UPI discipling staff
- expanding UPI's geographical reach to additional MLB cities
- emphasizing UPI's core ministry functions, with a specific focus on *training*
- leveraging strategic partnerships to support and enhance UPI's core ministry

Summary of Ministry Strategy Elements

UPI Staff Growth

Recruiting and training new UPI staff is the most critical element of the ministry's near term strategy. Tim Cash will lead the recruiting effort with input from the current team. Ideally, new staff will be younger (late 20s - 30s)—to insure a continued connection with the players—and have direct experience with MLB. The team is continually on the lookout for qualified candidates who could make a significant contribution to the ministry. Training of new team members requires 2-3 years of intentional mentoring, led by existing UPI staff in existing cities. As new staff members' relationships in the MLB community expand and their discipling capabilities are sharpened, they will be strategically relocated to cities where UPI enjoys greatest favor.

Geographic Expansion

As a relationship-based ministry, UPI maximizes its ministry impact when in *close proximity* to players and influencers within the MLB community. There is simply no better method of discipleship than a life-on-life approach. Currently, UPI has a physical presence in three MLB cities (Atlanta, Chicago, Phoenix) and has developed strong relationships in several others, including Kansas City, Milwaukee, and

San Diego. By 2013, UPI plans to expand its geographic footprint to two additional MLB cities.

For several years, UPI has focused heavily at the start of the MLB season on spring training venues, primarily in Florida and Arizona. The team plans to continue looking for opportunities to leverage that concentrated time with players for increased relationship-building and visibility for UPI.

Increased Core Ministry Emphasis

UPI's renewed emphasis on the core ministry functions of reaching, teaching and training has helped refocus the team strategically in their individual ministry efforts. UPI will continue to leverage outreach environments such as camps, mission trips, military trips, etc. as discipling opportunities for players. The staff's day-to-day efforts, however, will focus on the core.

Training players and influencers to impact others in their community is the most strategic of the three core functions. UPI staff have relatively short windows of face-to-face time with the players during the season. Conversely, a trained player or influencer has regular, daily interaction with his teammates and can model and disciple those around him more readily than the UPI staff. Therefore, training will be a critical thrust for UPI in the next 3-5 years.

Leveraging Strategic Partnerships

In each core ministry area, UPI has the opportunity to leverage strategic partnerships to provide increased access to players and influencers, teaching and discipleship resources, and increased credibility for the ministry.

> *Baseball Chapel* has been a partner of UPI for more than 20 years, providing UPI staff with new access to team clubhouses and a regular teaching platform in the weekly team chapel meetings.

> *Ravi Zacharias International Ministries* is a worldwide leader in Christian apologetics and related resources. UPI is exploring opportunities to leverage Ravi's teaching gifts and the RZIM's broad library of teaching and discipleship resources.

NavPress offers a broad range of publishing resources to UPI, both in existing content and publishing support for any new content UPI staff may create and wish to distribute.

Third Day, one of the leaders in Christian music today, has consistently supported UPI over the years and is open to exploring creative partnering ideas for outreach and ministry impact.

UPI Balanced Scorecard
The following is a tool to be used by the staff and may be helpful as a model for others in the ministry.

Discipleship/Development
Baseball Personnel Penetration
Gatekeeper Relationships
  Established
Additional Tools: Chapel /
  Studies
Outreach: Clinics / Intl./
  Military / etc.
	UPI Team
	Recruiting
	Training / Mentoring
	Teambuilding
	Compensation /
	  Benefits
	Balanced Lifestyle

Resources (Funding) Annual Operating Budget Donor Base Diversified Donor Relationships Cash Reserve Advancement	**Growth** New Staff Additions New Markets Strategic Partnerships (BC / Umpires, etc.) Website

The CORE of UPI is geared toward:
Reaching, teaching, training, and sending men in the professional baseball world.

Reaching – building relationships within the professional baseball community

    * Seeking to be used by God to lead others to Jesus.

Teaching – we teach the Word of God.
  *Believing that identity precedes activity.
  *Building guys up into their identity in Christ.

Training – Exposing guys to outreach ministry. Sharing our faith.
  *Locally – Nationally – Internationally - Militarily…
  *This is done with clinics, camps, and a variety of speaking opportunities.

Sending – Equipping guys to live out their faith authentically in their personal world.
  "Serving Christ through baseball" has been the motto.
  Sharing the greatest story ever told – through the greatest game ever played.

In 2008 the board voted yes to the plan. Titles were changed and chairs rearranged. I was named President/Founder and Tim Cash took the reins as Executive Director. Bryan Hickerson continues to serve as the Director of Military but added the important position of Director of Operations. Connie Johnson, who formerly held that position, became my Special Assistant before retiring in 2009. Mickey Weston continues to oversee the international portion of the work and was named Midwest Director, and Brian Hommel became the Southwest Director. New chairs, a new vision, and a great move of God.

The move honored the past while relishing the potential of the future. Much time was invested and the whole move was saturated with prayer. We praise God for directing us through this time of transition. It was not our desire to compare ourselves with other ministries but simply to honor God in our actions. We pray He has been honored.

My new role involves less day-to-day involvement in the operation of UPI, and Tim's role has increased in that area. I have to admit I had been doing a lot of thinking about what my new role would look like. After a full life of travel with friends all around the world, would I find myself spending my days behind a desk? Did I find my identity in what I had done? God answered all of these concerns. I now have the great privilege to work in the advancement area of UPI, counseling and developing the UPI alumni with the help of my talented friend, Chuck Yeager. I am able to share what God has done and what we feel He has called us to do in the future.

What does the future look like for UPI? None of us knows, but if the next thirty years looks like the past 30, it will be a great ride. God is all about sharing His love to a hurting world–your world. My challenge to you is to embrace your gifts, submit yourself to God, and go reach your world.

We are blessed and humbled to be called to be a part of what God is doing to build his kingdom.

"So, my dear brothers and sisters, be strong and steady, always enthusiastic about the Lord's work, for you know that nothing you do for the Lord is ever useless" (1 Corinthians 15:58 NLT).

It's Great to be alive because God is in control!

Action Points:

- Have you ever identified "your world"?
- Do you have a strategic plan for your life and ministry?
- Are you prepared to handle the transitions in your life?

Leadership

Any important discussion about leadership needs to include the consideration of one's motivation. Is it primarily production or principle driven? In business and in ministry both are important. However, in business productivity and profit determine the bottom line. Hopefully, principles are in place. In ministry biblical principles should lead, and production is God's business. With this in mind, I asked God to give me a principle-driven pattern to lead those He brought to work with UPI.

Often in ministry there is much hard work with few visible results. God may be using that time to mold and mature His workers in ministry. It may be His purpose to use the barrenness to strengthen faith and trust in Him. Productivity in ministry is not always something that can be managed and measured. If productivity is measured in lives changed, we may never know the full results in this life.

My desire was to lead by example. I wanted to be caring without being controlling. To keep others accountable without stifling creativity. To motivate with love instead of fear or guilt. To cultivate the workers' own style rather than having them mimic mine. Proverbs 16:9 says that man makes his plans but God directs his steps. My goal was to encourage our workers to use their gifts and abilities without hindering their personal journey with God.

I believe leadership involves creating tension for the purpose of exposure and transparency. Sometimes this means seeing rocks in the road and being there when others stumble. Preparation for ministry involves learning how to deal with adversity. A little tension can reveal motives, develop patience, and be great training for making godly decisions. I also believe good leaders teach others to accept responsibility for their own actions.

Early in the ministry I was challenged to surround myself with people who were better than me. When I look at the staff of UPI, I believe God has allowed that to happen. Tim, Mickey, Hick, and Brian; each adds a distinct signature to the ministry with his individual personalities, talents, and spiritual gifts. Each brings his own flavor to the ministry. It is a privilege to minister with such quality men.

The same thing is true for the UPI board of directors. Each man brings a different area of expertise to the table. With their prayerful guidance in finances, strategic planning, and vision, they have one thing in common: They each have a passion for advancing the cause of Christ. Each man who has served as board chairman lends his wisdom in setting policy as well as keeping the executive staff accountable to the policies of the ministry. Each man who has served on the board has had his own unique contribution. Larry Poyser was the initiator, Paul Refior gave UPI an international vision, Terry Harnish brought organization and accountability, and Randy Swanson has led through times of growth and challenge with a steady hand and godly wisdom. Randy has been the chair since 1993, and under his leadership the ministry has expanded as only God could allow.

Kent Fishel has been a UPI board member since the beginning of the ministry, so he understands its history. He is in full-time ministry and has a passion for reaching the world for Christ. He has a keen understanding of the Word of God and the need for prayer. Randy, in addition to strong leadership, has a background in finance and has put in place solid principles of stewardship. In recent years Scott Sanderson and Cal Eldred were added to the board. As former major leaguers they bring the perspective of the players. Recently the addition of Atlanta businessmen Tom Tabor and Jay Foxworthy gives us a rounded understanding of God's direction today.

They have advised, encouraged, and protected the staff. Many times Randy and I have sat over coffee as he listened to me pour out my heart. Sometimes a man needs another man to discuss issues and gain perspective, a man who can be trusted with confidences and who will offer godly advice. There have been tough times, even times when I have felt like giving up. Randy has a way of understanding with gentleness and firmness, and his words have been like a cool drink after a long race. I am deeply grateful for his leadership.

The principle of surrounding yourself with men who are better than you is one I have tried to pass on. According to Proverbs 15:22, "Plans fail for lack of counsel, but with many advisors they succeed." When others ask for guidance when starting a new ministry or a new phase of life, my advice is to form a board of godly people to provide wisdom and accountability. One such man who asked is Kraig Cabe, director for Northern Indiana of the Fellowship of Christian Athletes (FCA). He sent this e-mail:

> When I was in the process of starting Northern Indiana FCA several years ago, I approached you about any thoughts you had on putting together a local board of advisors, and I'll never forget your words of wisdom. You simply said that there are two basic ways to put together a board: 1) The wealthiest people you know or 2) The godliest people you know. You said you would take godliness over wealth every time.
>
> I put together our board with that thought specifically in mind, and I have found that there are many out there that can support our ministry financially, but there are fewer who can offer biblical counsel in an appropriate, timely manner. Because of your advice, we have avoided many of the pitfalls associated with not-for-profit boards and have grown this ministry because we have been able to avoid distractions and keep focused on the most important thing: serving Jesus Christ.
>
> Thank you for sharing your wisdom. The first board I ever witnessed in action was the board I assembled (with the Lord's help through you), and it has been a joy to serve with them.

With godly men serving on the UPI board and a great staff working alongside me in this ministry, I desired to lead in a godly way as the director of the ministry. Added staff brought both blessing and responsibility. Coming from a coaching background, I had some ideas on leadership, but ministry was a new ball game. My coaching philosophy had been that people were more important than programs and programs were more important than winning, although winning was important. Would that philosophy transfer to ministry?

In seeking to find the right leadership style, I looked to the Word of God and other ministries for examples. I have always admired the Billy Graham Association and the way the ministry was handled. I greatly respected the integrity and reputation of the Graham organization and wanted to learn anything from them that could apply to UPI. In many ways UPI has followed the model of that great ministry. Several times while traveling through North Carolina, I met with John Akers, one of the leaders in the organization, to seek his counsel.

But pro athletes are a unique group. They have reached the highest level of success in their sport. Some of that is God-given ability, and some of it is mental toughness and a fierce desire to win. The men who are full-time UPI staff all came out of a background in professional baseball. They know the game, they are highly motivated, and they have a competitive nature. Each has the heart of a champion. Each has been called by God into ministry, but I knew that some of that competitive spirit needed to be reshaped.

First, I realized that these men were young when they started with UPI, and I sensed my role was to lead them like a family member. I wanted to let them know they were loved and that I believed in them. I needed to show this with my actions as well as words. When they were confronted with tough times, regardless of how they responded, they needed to know they were loved. I believe this is the way Christ leads us and the way He called me to lead.

Second, I needed to find a way to lead while continuing to be heavily involved in the ministry myself. I hit my knees again, asking God to show me how He wanted me to lead. Although each man on staff is different, they all have a great work ethic and they were eager to begin. I did not want to lead with a performance-based or discipline-based style. I wanted to lead by encouraging each man to be led by the Holy Spirit. Although I understood that God had placed me in this position of authority and that policies are necessary, I wanted to see the men walk by faith rather than by rules. The work belongs to God, and I was just one of His workers.

Third, I wondered if the same training would work for all of them. They were each unique, with different gifts and abilities. How could I help each one transition from the game of baseball to baseball ministry? The Lord seemed to impress the need to encourage them to develop their own style of ministry rather than training them to follow my example. In other words, they needed to be who God created them to be, not a clone of me. They needed to keep their eyes on the goal while listening to the voice of the Holy Spirit. They would need this direction for the days ahead when they moved away from the home office.

Miles Stanford said, "We might consider some familiar names of believers whom God obviously brought to maturity and used for His glory—such as Pierson, Chapman, Tauler, Moody, Goforth, Mueller, Taylor, Watt, Trumbull, Meyer, Murray, Havergal, Guyon, Mabie, Gordon, Hyde, Mantle, McCheyne, McConkey, Deck, Paxon, Stoney, Saphir, Carmichael, and Hopkins. The average for these [men] was fifteen years after they entered their life work before they began to know the Lord Jesus as their Life and ceased trying to work for Him and began allowing Him to be their all in all and do His work through them. This is not to discourage us in any way, but to help us settle down with our sights on eternity, by faith 'apprehending that for which also we are apprehended of Christ Jesus, pressing toward the mark for the prize of the high calling of God in Christ Jesus'" (Philippians 3:12b paraphrased).

I wondered if there was any way to cut down those fifteen years. According to Rob Yandian, "Those who advance too quickly because of their own efforts have found the descent to be faster than the ascent."

The following is the plan that I believe was right for training the UPI staff. It is the Be, See, Flee, Be, and Plea Plan. This plan varied with each man, based on the amount of time with them and the understanding they each brought to ministry.

The Be, See, Flee, Plea, and Be Plan
The UPI Leadership Training

BE (3-6 months)
This is a time for the leaders in training to be quiet before God and learn from Him. It is a challenge for any man to learn who he is without the pressure to perform, to slow down and take time to hear from God.

SEE (3-12 months)
A time of observation that can overlap with the BE portion.

I remember speaking a number of years ago to a leader of a large athletic ministry. His take was that, although the pro athletes bring something to the ministry table, he was not going to consider them for ministry positions. I thought about his statement but took a different approach. I felt UPI needed to have former athletes on staff to relate to the culture and lifestyle of baseball. Athletes are dedicated and not afraid to work. Athletes want to perform.

Pro baseball is basically a second shift, blue-collar job with white-collar executive pay. Most games are played at night; that makes it second shift. They work weekends, and the fans do not typically see all the physical work that takes place before any pitch is thrown or ball hit. These athletes are dedicated and not afraid to work. Athletes want to perform. Some balk, however, at quick and non-understanding evaluation, the kind that baseball fans and management do almost everyday.

During the "Be" and "See" portion of my leadership style, there were times when I could have done the work instead of asking the staff person. I needed to learn to delegate, as well as to allow others to experience victory. There were times I sensed an individual needed to perform, to have success, and to sense his worth. I would give an athlete an assignment and always praise his work. If the job needed adjustments, there were other times and ways to make them. I think each of us wanted ministry evaluation and pressure to be different from what was experienced in baseball.

I wanted to see how staff responded to all types of work at different times and with different assignments.

During this time I observed such things as:

- How they handle times of inactivity
- How they handle stress
- How they respond to adversity
- How they manage their time
- How they relate to their spouse and children
- If they have a need to be in control
- What interests they have
- Their level of contentment
- If they get proper rest
- How they respond to criticism
- How they respond to authority (A true servant does not have a problem with authority. He can take commands and, although he may not agree, he still performs the task with a good heart.)
- How they handle money
- How they direct their competitive nature
- How they value integrity
- What opinions they offer
- How they respond to gifts (financial and spiritual)
- How much of a team player they are
- Their transitioning process from player to minister
- Whether they take responsibility or blame
- How they handle fear
- How they handle loneliness
- Are they patient?
- Are they loyal?
- What are their weaknesses?
- How they handle the Word of God (as a fine surgeon or as a demolition driver)
- Strengths
- Sensitivity to others
- Moodiness
- Motivation

During this time of observation we work on the following:

- Office: a time to learn organizational skills
- Meetings: a time to discuss personal needs, ministry policies, and questions about life in general
- Prayer: a time to commit ministry concerns to the Lord
- Personal Worship: a time to listen to music, read, meditate on, and respond to God's Word personally
- Study: a time for looking into the truths of the Word.

FLEE (3-6 months)

I separate myself from them intentionally to see how they respond on their own. This is a tough time as they struggle with getting started, scheduling, organizing, prioritizing, executing, and balancing work and rest.

PLEA

A time to reconnect with each man and listen to his heart. To ask for forgiveness for leaving him alone and to help him understand the purpose in the process. It is a time to review and evaluate, to better understand individual gifts and ministry styles, and to encourage dependence on God rather than people. It is a time for each man to do business with God and find out his uniqueness.

BE

This is the time for him to go out, in the power of the Holy Spirit, and BE who God has called him to be, expressing his unique gifts, calling, and personality to the baseball culture.

"It is good for me that I was afflicted so that I may learn your decrees" (Psalm 119:71).

"Effective leaders, at all levels of leadership, maintain a learning posture throughout life. Effective leaders who are productive over a lifetime have a dynamic ministry philosophy that evolves continually from the interplay of three major factors: biblical dynamics, personal gifts, and situational dynamics."

Dr. J. Robert Clinton

"When you give a man something to do, don't tell him how to do it. Just tell him what you want done and he may surprise you with his ingenuity."
General George S. Patton

Typically we learn leadership styles from the leaders in our own lives, such as teachers, coaches, ministers, or parents. Also we may have observed political or military leaders. But God gives us the freedom to lead in a different way. My goal for the men God brought under my leadership was to help them become God-fearing, God-dependent dreamers and thinkers who meet regularly with God and wait for His direction and confirmation. It was not my goal to be the model of a sports minister. I wanted their fingerprints all over their work, not mine. I did not want them to follow me; I wanted them to follow God.

"The measure of leadership is not the quality of the head, but the tone of the body."
Max DuPree

A major part of spiritual leadership is learning that God is in control. It is learning how to handle fear when faced with unexpected situations or tough decisions. When we forget that God is in control, we can be controlled by fear. There will be frightening times, and fear can sometimes be good. Fear can be crippling or it can drive us to our knees. The Lord told Joshua to be strong and courageous because He would be with him. We may feel lonely, but never are we alone.

On a personal note, in the beginning of the ministry I thought that each day needed to be a day of spectacular insight, revelation, and challenge in order to really make a difference. I learned that often the most important thing we can do is just show up. If we go where God sends, He does the rest.

As the director of UPI, I have never seen my role to be that of a Bible teacher. There are many Bible teachers who are far better than I am. I have told the staff that if I am a teacher, it is an elementary school teacher. My desire is to come alongside them to encourage them, help work though issues, and deal with exceptions. I learned early that a large part of leadership is handling those blessed exceptions.

I did not want to control these men or smother them. I wanted them to be real, to use their gifts, and I wanted to give them room to make mistakes and learn from them. As a coach I often told my players to play for an audience of One. That was also my desire for the staff. I wanted to be available but stay out of the way so they would follow that One.

"Because leadership is necessarily an exercise of authority," writes Eugene Peterson in his introduction to 2 Corinthians in *The Message,* "it easily shifts into an exercise of power. But the minute it does that, it begins to inflict damage on both the leader and the led. Paul, studying Jesus, had learned a kind of leadership in which he managed to stay out of the way so that others could deal with God without having to go through him."

Hubert Humphrey once said, "Like many things in our national life, we miscalculated. We overestimated our ability to control events, which is one of the great dangers of a great power. Power tends to be a substitute for judgment and wisdom."

I knew I had been given a humbling task in attempting to train leaders. Over the years I have compiled a list of principles from many sources that inspire me. I keep this list close to me—on my desk, in my Bible, on my laptop—as constant reminders, and I have attempted to pass these ideals on to the staff. It usually did not happen in a formal setting but during informal conversations on the phone, by e-mail, or while on the road. Here is that list:

- Be positive; Caleb saw the potential when others did not.
- To compare is an error.
- God is in control.
- Heart, vision, and passion are vital for a godly leader.
- Always choose character over ability or experience.
- FLO = Be faithful, loyal, and obedient.
- In ministry we are both ministers and administrators.
- Is my yes a yes? – James 5:12.
- Be strong and courageous – Joshua 1:8.
- Be bold – Psalm 16:8.
- Have a critical eye rather than a critical spirit. It's an attitude issue.

- Our thinking determines our emotions which determine our actions.
- Love equals obedience.
- Dependency is built on trust.
- When wronged, our best defense attorney is Jesus.
- Accept responsibility.
- You may be hated without reason – John 15:25.
- I am small, but He is big.
- When you have a setback, sit back before you come back.
- S.T.A.R. (Straight Thinkers Accept Responsibility) = Maturity (devised by Jerry Price).
- We are all just broken lambs.
- Develop persistence and resistance—persistence to persevere and resistance to mediocrity.
- Develop discipline and dedication.
- There is a difference between power and influence.
- Slow cooking > more tender. Time is your friend, not your enemy.
- Stay HOT = humble, obedient, and teachable.
- Leadership style: David, Saul, or Absalom (from *The Tale of Three Kings* by Gene Edwards)
- Wash feet = attitude of a servant.
- We can choose to be bitter or better.
- Motivated by money or ministry – Matthew 6:33.
- Practice quick repentance – Isaiah 14:12.
- There is a fine line between confidence and arrogance.
- Learn to delegate.
- Allow people to fail. Failure is a great teacher.
- Emotions are good, but they are spice, not meat.
- Learn to listen to the older saints—they have battle scars.
- Be an example; leave a legacy.
- Work within your gifts.

Vince Nauss, director of Baseball Chapel, once told me that one of the pitfalls of having men in the field is that they can take personal ownership of their ministry and forget they are part of a bigger picture. I have seen this happen and understand the tension between sending men out to minister in their own style while maintaining the sense of family and unity within this diverse group. I have not always succeeded in this.

Vince and I both agree that four important qualities of a leader are humility, purpose, vision, and communication. Humility means never letting pride deny you the opportunity to serve those who work with you. It is important never to lose sight of the purpose for which God has called you and the vision He has given you. Communication is relating that vision to those you work with and challenging them to stay on course.

I have made some major mistakes in leadership. At times I have misunderstood motives or blindly trusted others. God tends to fill in the cracks of my mistakes by bringing others alongside staff members.

One fall day at an International Sports Coalition meeting I remember being asked about my failures. I had the opportunity to meet with Eddie Waxer and Paul Eshleman, two men in ministry I greatly admired. As we sat in a small room in Houston, Texas, I was ready to share all the great things UPI had done. The first question they asked me was, "In what ways has UPI failed?" It caught me off guard. But now I understand that our honest mistakes help shape us. Our failures build into us a greater compassion for others and a deeper dependency on prayer.

One final area of leadership training is to involve players in missions trips. The baseball players we take are at various levels in their commitment to Christ. Some are "kites" and others are "bricks." Some fly with Jesus and others are bricks and have to be carried. I asked God to show me how to develop a team of kites. I challenge anyone reading this book to seriously ask God to show you who those men are in your life that He sees as faithful, and invest in them. Be part of the wind beneath their wings. One of my favorite quotes is: "We can spend our life anywhere, but where will we invest it?"

A leader is just a sheep in shepherds' clothing. My prayer is that every life touched by the ministry of UPI would not turn to gold, but to clay, easy for Jesus to mold to conform to Himself.

It's Great to be alive because God is in control!

Action Points:

- Many of you who are reading this chapter are very likely in a leadership position—whether in a company, a ministry, with a child or a disciple. Have you ever intentionally thought out your plan for leadership?

- Have you thought about your transition into the next chapter of life? How might your thinking change as a result of noting some of the issues dealt with in this chapter?

- How are you spending your life? Are you investing it for the Kingdom of God?

"With man this is impossible,
but with God all things are possible."
(Jesus, Matthew 19:26)

For more information, contact
Unlimited Potential Inc.
P.O. Box 1355
Warsaw, IN 46581-1355
www.upi.org